international interiors 7

international interiors 7

Jeremy Myerson

Co-ordinating researcher
Jennifer Hudson

LAURENCE KING

Published 2000 by Laurence King Publishing
an imprint of Calmann & King Ltd
71 Great Russell Street
London WC1B 3BN
Tel: +44 20 7831 6351
Fax: +44 20 7831 8356
e-mail: enquiries@calmann-king.co.uk
www.laurence-king.com

A catalogue record for this book is available from
the British Library.

ISBN 1 85669 183 7

Design: Price Watkins

Printed in Hong Kong

Frontispiece: Reichstag Plenary building, Berlin (see page 202).
Photograph: Richard Bryant/Arcaid.

Acknowledgements. The author and the publishers would like to
thank all the designers and architects involved and the photographers
whose work is reproduced. The following photographic credits are
given, with page numbers in parentheses:
Terge Agnalt (194–7); Luis Astn (10 right, 36–7); Paul Barker (21);
Gabriele Basilico (120–3); Crtsy BDG McColl (218 top, 219 top);
Gunter Bieringer (144–5, 147); Bitter Bredt Fotografie (174, 176,
178, 179 bottom); Catherine Bogert (11, 46–9); Tom Bonner
(55, 92–7); Richard Bryant-Arcaid (22 right,42–5, 82–7, 202–6 top,
207); Friedrich Busam-Architekturphoto (102–5, 177, 179 top);
Alessandro Cecchini (106–9); Benny Chan (12–19); Niall Clutton
(138–43); Peter Cook-VIEW (168–71); Whitney Cox (212–13);
Giorgio Dettori (98–101); Peter Durant-arcblue (20, 22 left, 23, 110
right, 112–19); Klaus Frahm (54 right, 88–91); Jeff Goldberg–ESTO
(68–70 top, 71); Roland Halbe-artur (72-–5); Michael Heinrich
(222–5); Timothy Hursely (226–9); Elliott Kaufman (214–15);
Angelo Kaunat (146); Christian Kerber (80–1); Michael Kleinberg
(70 bottom); Toshiyuki Kobayashi (186–9); Dolores Marat (164–7);
Ian McKinnell (148–51); Michael Moran (32–5); Michael O'Callahan
(24–7); Tomio Ohashi (173, 216–18 bottom, 219 bottom, 220–21);
Paul Ratigan (56–9); Tuca Reines (111, 161–3); Christian Richters
(175); Cervin Robinson (172 left, 180–5); Cees Roelofs Crtsy Interpolis
(50–3); Martin Schodder (190–3); Crtsy Claudio Silvestrin (60–3);
Doug Snower Photography (125–9); Timothy Soar (156–9);
Margeritha Spillutini (110 left, 134–7); Hisao Suzuki (172 right,
208–11); Paul Tyagi (54 left, 64–7); Philip Vile (198–201); Alexander
Van Berge (28–31); Marley Von Sternberg (152–5); Jonty Wilde
(130–3); Willebrand Photographie (10 left, 38–41); Adrian Wilson
(76–9); Nigel Young (206 bottom).

contents

introduction

'I will always prefer a perfect slice of bread with olive oil to a butter-fat croissant that merely gives the illusion of luxury…'

Interior designer, Rena Dumas of Hermès

The seventh edition of *International Interiors* provides an insight into the art of the interior designer at a special moment in time, the end of a century in which the interior design profession could be said to have successfully laid claim to a definitive territory which is neither too close to interior decoration nor indistinguishable from architecture.

It does so through the medium of 48 work, leisure, retail and public projects from around the world, a collection of schemes that reflects current interests and preoccupations among some of the most thoughtful practitioners and adventurous clients on the international scene.

The projects selected for this publication were largely completed in a two-year period between autumn 1997 and autumn 1999, giving an eve-of-millennium flavour to the design work featured. But the *fin de siècle* mood is markedly different from 100 years ago. Back in 1900, as designers anticipated the impact that the telephone, typewriter and light bulb might have on the office interior, for example, or explored the way the motor car might influence leisure, the frenzy of anticipation was reflected in the prevailing Art Nouveau style which featured swirling, asymmetric forms that reflected an excited world of flux.

In 2000, the world is no less in flux as internet technologies reshape everything from the corporate organization to the high-street store, but designers are contemplating it in a rather more measured and less excited way. If the twentieth century has taught designers anything at all, it is that unconstrained production leaves scars, identity is more than skin-deep, and that all forms of design – especially those related to physical environment – are tinged with social ethics and ecology. Sustainable interior design for many is not only about quality of life but also renewable resources.

Indeed, the search for genuine quality, as opposed to superficial opulence, underscores many of the design projects in this book. New workplaces reflect the making of more humane, collaborative and productive environments, rather than those driven by corporate hubris and based on corporate icons. Leisure interiors are using abstract forms, bright colours and modest materials to engage, not just impress. Retail marketplaces are reintroducing narrative forms of architecture and public buildings are implementing more democratic design solutions, with one aim: to create quality experiences that are inclusive, rather than grand monolithic statements that are remote.

Rena Dumas' preference for simple, olive oil-dipped bread over the bloated butter-fat croissant reflects an ethos focused on communicating a sense of quality by getting the details right: this is regarded as more sustainable than creating an appearance of luxuriousness which is little more than a mirage. As a design approach, it often manifests itself in use of materials, as in Dumas' own Hermès shop in Lille, with its leather-clad staircase and panelled walls of copper-toned French cherrywood; or in Yasmine Mahmoudieh's SAS Royal Hotel renovation in Copenhagen, with its Danish maple, coloured glass and local fabrics; or in MacCormac Jamieson Prichard's Ruskin Library at Lancaster University, with its slate, English oak and leather.

The materials are often local because creating a local sense of place is becoming more important to interior designers the more the world shrinks. It seems the antidote to the global media village is ethnic pattern, vibrant colour and patinated materials from the lignite brick to the pebble mosaic. In the case of Oslo's new Gardermoen Airport, designed by Aviaplan, the antidote to bland international terminal design is an abundance of Norwegian wood.

Of course, some projects revel in the technologies of the future: Nicholas Grimshaw's Mexican computer centre and Ellen Sander's Dutch Media Plaza are both straight from an early Stanley Kubrick film set. But other schemes seem determined to turn back the clock. In the case of Eric Kuhne's extraordinary Bluewater retail development in Kent,

UK, the army of artesans, sculptors, craftsmen and ironsmiths from all over Britain required to build such a decorative scheme – with more than 50 pieces of civic art – succeeded in revitalizing some crafts neglected for a generation or more. Infused with the myths and legends of English landscape and literature, Bluewater goes vividly against the flow of the cool new modernism of late-1990s urban culture. But it is not the only evidence of a backlash against designer minimalism in retailing; even the fashion temples are breaking out of the mould.

Projects from 15 different countries, including The Netherlands, Spain, Mexico, Austria, Denmark, Italy, Brazil, France, Malaysia, Finland, Norway and Japan, feature in *International Interiors 7*. The lion's share of the schemes are American, British and German, reflecting the 'fast company' culture and innovative workplace design on the east and west coasts of the US; the restless invention of retail and leisure design in the UK; and the serious investment in quality public environments in Germany.

Predictions of an end to the nation-state were part of the general forecast for the twenty-first century. But national and indeed local qualities, manifested in the most minutely-observed details, remain an important aspect of interior design practice. It seems that the more the world is wired through cyberspace, the greater the need for interior designers to preserve the essential human connections through physical structure, visual form and user experience.

1 work

1.7

1.5

Cellular offices are making a comeback and 'hoteling' is in retreat as organizations provide more personal places to work.

Project dens, boulevard cafés, retro diners, even basketball courts reflect the office for living in, and not just working in.

Light and colour are used to introduce sci-fi theatricality to workplaces that trade on a high-tech image.

Even call centres and computer centres show their creative side as metaphors shape their interior landscape.

Flexibility is more than moveable screens – it permeates the culture of the cordless work environment.

The rubber deck and the glass-bridge walkway reinstate the public promenade in the corporate office.

Cyber-companies in waterfront warehouses are using the robustness of an earlier industrial age to show their strength.

Whether oak-lined sanctuary or stripped-down studio, some workplaces are quieter and calmer than ever before.

1.1 **tbwa/chiat/day** los angeles, usa

TBWA/Chiat/Day, the creative brain behind Apple's 'Think Different' campaign and much other award-winning work, is the largest advertising agency on America's west coast. It is also the best known in terms of its espousal of innovative workplace design, having utilized the skills of Frank Gehry in the past. This latest project – a spectacular relocation to an entire advertising 'city' in the Playa Vista area of Los Angeles – not only marks a departure from Gehry's famous 'Binocular' building in Venice but a move away from the work-anywhere, or 'hoteling', concept which was the major operational premise of the Venice office.

Designed by Clive Wilkinson, the new scheme unites the entire agency – more than 350 people – within a giant renovated warehouse building that is reached via a sculptural, metal-clad gatehouse. In terms of scale and ambition, it marks the most complete adoption of the office-as-city metaphor yet seen, while offering some of the most imaginative material solutions. Entry to the 'city' from the gatehouse (which features a reception area and gallery for the agency's work) is via two pedestrian 'tubes', each 50 feet in length. These capsule-like entrance bridges evoke the embarkation tubes of aircraft. Once inside, the vista opens to an entire small-city environment with multiple levels, green park space, landmark structures, an 'irregular' skyline, distinct neighbourhoods, café spaces, light wells, even a basketball court.

A 'main street' bissects the ground floor, and flying bridges and ramps connect the mezzanines, within a soaring space that rises to 27 feet in height. The creative department is placed right at the centre of the agency, its personnel housed in mechanistic 'cliff dwellings' – bright yellow constructions of steel, concrete and metal decking – on either side of the high street. 'Hoteling' proved unpopular with TBWA/Chiat/Day staff in Venice, so the agency has this time given people their own personal place at which to work, together with facilities to promote teamworking. No single adaptable workstation product existed on the market to combine personal and team needs, so after detailed research a custom design was developed by Clive Wilkinson and his client for the 500 units needed. Manufactured by Steelcase, these metal and wood workstations, called *Nests*, encircle the city centre and accommodate project teams in office neighbourhoods. Project dens, which are ethereal full-height enclosures realized as tent structures, are interspersed within a thrillingly generous layout that aims to maximize creative collaboration while at the same time ensuring everyone has their own home.

Designer: **Clive Wilkinson**. Commissioning Client: **TBWA/Chiat/Day**. Total Floor Space: **120,000 square feet**. Number of Levels: **3**. Contract Cost: **Confidential**. Completed: **December 1998**.

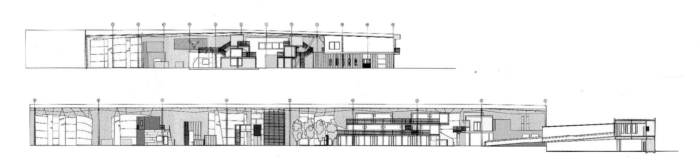

above The cross-section and longitudinal section reveal a workplace modelled on the idea of a complete city.
opposite View of the stacked metal 'cliff dwellings' from the main street which even has its own traffic, albeit stationary.

above Surfboards and classic modern furniture signal a
consciously creative welcome in the gallery-style gatehouse,
which is the reception area for the agency.

opposite View from the gatehouse reception desk down the twin
pedestrian tubes through which everyone must travel to
reach the building. The idea is to suggest arrival in the office
city from the narrow capsule of an aircraft.

left Panoramic view of the main street piazza at
TBWA/Chiat/Day, complete with planting, street furniture
and British red telephone box.
below Looking down into the agency work areas where
Apple's 'Think Different' campaign was created.

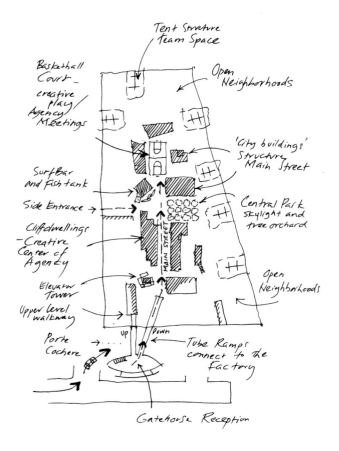

Tent Structure
Team Space

Basketball
Court –
creative
play/
Agency
Meetings

Open
Neighborhoods

'City buildings'
Structure
Main Street

SurfBar
and Fish tank

Side Entrance →

Central Park
skylight and
tree orchard

Cliffdwellings
– Creative
Center of
Agency

Elevator
Tower

Open
Neighborhoods

Upper level
walkway

Porte
Cochere

UP   Down

Tube Ramps
connect to the
factory

Gatehouse Reception

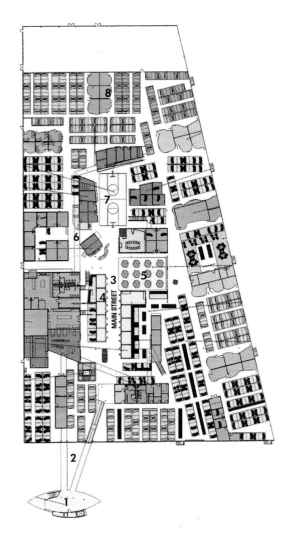

key
1 gatehouse reception
2 ramp
3 main street
4 cliff dwelling
5 central park
6 surf bar
7 basketball court
8 project den tent structure

above View of the art studio at the rear of the 'cliff dwellings'. A cafeteria and conference rooms can be reached on the mezzanine level.

opposite Full-height tensile structures create project dens. Clustered workstations were specially designed for the project by the architect. Called *Nests*, they were made by Steelcase to meet both group and individual needs.

left The concept sketch and ground-floor plan show the scale of the facility.

The Whitehouse Ruskin Collection is a large archive of books and papers by or about the Victorian savant John Ruskin (1819–1900). For many years sited in an annexe to an educational foundation on the Isle of Wight, the archive was in need of a secure and controlled environment. A new home was proposed at Lancaster University, which offered an established programme of Ruskin studies and was also happily near to a companion Ruskin collection kept at Brantwood on Lake Coniston. The site for the new library was a former bowling green on an escarpment facing Morecambe Bay. There MacCormac Jamieson Prichard's new library building sits like a symbolic western gateway to the university.

The Ruskin Library's interior is first glimpsed as a secluded inner sanctum sandwiched between two elliptical outer walls. The effect is one of security dramatically expressed. At night the library acts like a beacon, its gleaming interior cupped and shielded by the curved walls. Access is through a bronze-clad porch that opens out into a double-height entrance hall where a large, red, free-standing box dominates the space. This is one of two archives depicted as huge treasure chests which rise up from a lower basement area through a floor of slate and glass, part of a repeating theme of a stylized lagoon disgorging its treasure. The aquatic associations persist, from dark walls sealed with linseed oil to a tall shuttered window that bears a semi-translucent abstraction of a Ruskin daguerreotype taken from a portal of St Mark's in Venice.

A reading room for eight readers typifies the high quality of the interior, with its solid crafted chairs of English oak upholstered in leather and its oak-framed tables inlaid with walnut. In fact, once you have left the drama of the exterior behind, the variety of materials and finishes of the Ruskin Library's rich interior are what mark it out as special. These materials also have a practical purpose: this major archive is passively conditioned, with the masonry walls and large air volumes acting as heat sinks.

Architect: **MacCormac Jamieson Prichard**.

Commissioning Client: **Lancaster University**. Total Floor Space: **722 square metres**. Number of Levels: **3**. Contract Cost: **£1.9 million**. Completed: **November 1997**.

above The glowing inner sanctum glimpsed between two elliptical outer walls. The white concrete-and-marble composition with green bands recalls Ruskin's fascination with Venetian and Tuscan construction.
opposite Arts and Crafts reading room.
below Section.

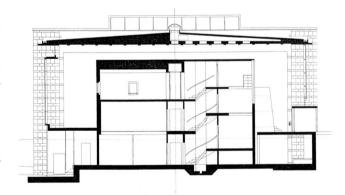

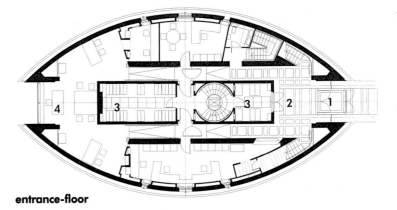

entrance-floor

from left South gallery; entrance view of the archive encased in oak-bound Venetian-red treasure chest; dignified reading room with leather and oak furniture.
above entrance-floor plan.
below first-floor plan.

key
1 porch
2 entrance
3 archive spaces
4 reading
5 void over reading
6 void over entrance
7 meeting
8 gallery

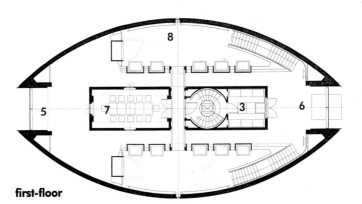

first-floor

Call centres have been described as 'the sweatshops of the twenty-first century'. But this project comes up smelling of roses – largely, one suspects, because it is a call centre and marketing office for a florist business selling blooms by telephone. Calyx & Corolla started life in one small cramped room in 1988. Within a decade, it had grown into a $20-million enterprise. Its new workplace on two floors of the China Basin Landing Building in San Francisco, a former industrial warehouse, has toughness and fragrance all rolled into one design package.

There is a pleasing tension between the robust fabric of the original building and the abstract garden design metaphor that gives the interior scheme by Studios Architecture its charm. A green, cut-pile carpet acts as a lawn; flower arrangements are designed and tested in a 'potting shed' and distributed throughout the space; an open conference area is defined by a stucco garden wall. Concrete blocks and ceiling slabs, wood slattings, awnings and trellis are used to embellish the theme.

The upper floor is dedicated to the call centre operators who handle up to 14,000 calls a day from customers in peak season. Their numbers fluctuate – from 25 to 150,

depending on the time of year – so open-plan space and systems furniture are flexibly organized along a 200-foot window-wall promenade. The sixth-floor marketing and executive area is different in function and style: this is where the 18 different seasonal catalogues are produced, so individual offices and meeting spaces predominate. The scheme was executed swiftly, in just six weeks, but it nevertheless reflects a thoughtful approach. In an age of robot-style telephone centres, this one is refreshingly human in tone.
Designer: **Studios Architecture**. Commissioning Client: **Calyx & Corolla**. Total Floor Space: **25,000 square feet**. Number of Levels: **2**. Contract Cost: **Confidential**. Completed: **November 1997**.

opposite Second-floor call centre operation (above) and sixth-floor conference room (below).
below Second-floor and sixth-floor plans.

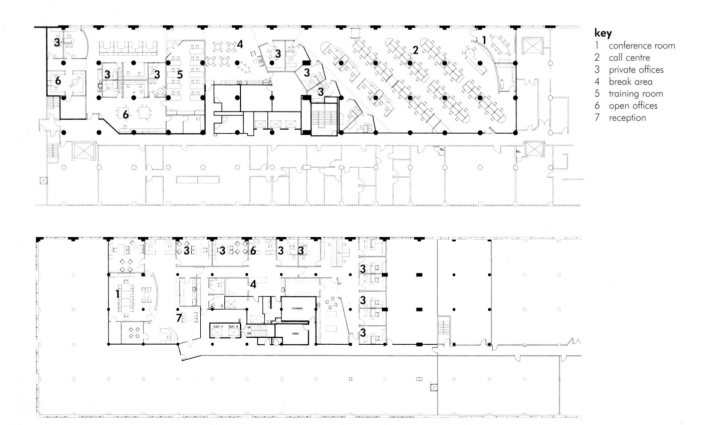

key
1   conference room
2   call centre
3   private offices
4   break area
5   training room
6   open offices
7   reception

above Break area.

opposite The abstract garden design metaphor lends this seasonal business the flavour of the potting shed.

Media Plaza is a futuristic government information centre in Utrecht aimed at making senior decision-makers in Dutch industry more aware of the importance of the information superhighway. Designed by Ellen Sander of Sander Architecten, its purpose is to take managers out of their every-day working lives and encourage them to stop and think about the technologies of the future. Media Plaza's location in a small hall within the extensive and rather unattractive Jaarbeurs trade-fair complex made it imperative that the interior should deliver an out-of-this-world experience, and that is precisely what Sander has achieved.

Industrialists enter the showcase by walking through a giant tube clad with stainless-steel mesh. Its laminated glass-bridge walkway is lit from below by glass fibre cables. This is not a passage entered lightly, and it gives a sense of encountering a different future. The tube leads visitors into a great hall in which there is a deliberate sense of movement achieved with running neon in the flooring, shifting lights, and a stainless-steel ceiling shifting slowly through space in a wave. Even the toilet block is an experience in itself, as glass elements, stainless-steel washbasins, internet screens set into the floor and water reflections on the wall indicate that this is no ordinary corporate office facility.

The technical nerve centre of Media Plaza is a sculptural 'highway shuttle' designed to accommodate business presentations to small groups (20 people maximum). The idea is of a space shuttle making a quick trip to another galaxy. Visitors emerge from the shuttle to encounter a virtual marketplace offering hands-on display of the wares of the electronic superhighway within 'cells' of stretched transparent rubber. An oval-shaped skybar with padded walls of blood-red velvet provides a sanctuary to relax in after the exertions of the imagination. This is a scheme that pushes hard at the spatial and technological boundaries in a bid to open minds to new opportunities. As Ellen Sander argues, 'architecture is not a way of building, but a way of thinking.'

Designers: **Sander Architecten**. Commissioning Client: **Media Plaza Foundation**. Total Floor Space: **2,000 square metres**. Number of Levels: **1**. Contract Cost: **US$3 million**. Completed: **May 1997**.

opposite Entrance to the Media Plaza is via this dramatic glass bridge lit from below by glass fibre cables.

below The floor plan reflects the visitor's 'journey' through the environment, with a 'highway shuttle' for futuristic business presentations at the centre.

key
1 entrance tube
2 internet plaza
3 foyer
4 highway shuttle
5 arcade
6 skybar
7 catwalk

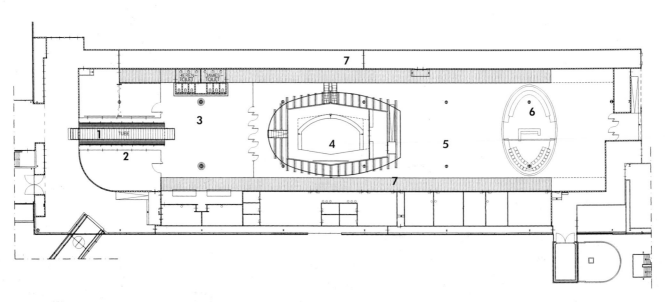

opposite Views of the foyer with its shimmering neon floor patterns and sci-fi elements.
right Even the toilet facilities reflect the theme of new technological horizons, with internet connections complementing custom-designed basins.

1.5 `barnesandnoble.com` new york, usa

Matching the physical work environment to the fast-changing needs of a virtual business is one of the emerging challenges of the age for the interior designer. Following the internet success of amazon.com, established US bookseller Barnes and Noble created its own web division, barnesandnoble.com. This has grown rapidly, prompting a move by its web development group to a new office on the 11th floor of the New York Port Authority Building. The task for Anderson Architects was to work within the straitjacket of a tight schedule, limited budget, complex technical requirements and existing structural grid to create a workspace that would be dynamic in use and flexible in approach.

The resulting scheme is as tough-minded in its thinking as it is robust in its finishes, which range from raw and blackened steel, and exposed and painted concrete to maple plywood, black chalkboard, translucent fibreglass panels and clear green acrylic. The designers have recognized the organization's three main levels of hierarchy within the plan while minimizing their effect. There are, for example, perimeter offices for executives but these alternate with open bays with oversized windows that preserve views of the Hudson River and upper and lower Manhattan for all.

Managers work in boldly painted 'worm-shaped' offices that slither between existing structural columns. The third level of hierarchy belongs to the team members whose open workstations can be viewed through a forest of dark-painted concrete columns. Above, the open ductwork of the exposed ceiling is lit by linear fluorescent-strip uplighters.

In the reception area visitors are met by a customized desk and metal-screen garage door. They then follow a circulation route lit by glowing acrylic disks and intense spots to an open area outside a state-of-the-art network operations centre which forms the heart of the project. Clad in galvanized metal, this appears to 'float' in what was originally the truck pit of the Port Authority Building's 11th-floor loading dock. A viewport offers flickering glimpses of the network systems that are the brain of the business. To the north is a high-tech main conference room with glowing acrylic media cabinet and custom conference table wired for video-conferencing and multimedia presentations. In a setting once associated with maritime trade and wealth, barnesandnoble.com is charting a new course through cyberspace.

Designers: **Anderson Architects**. Commissioning Client: **Barnes and Noble Inc.** Total Floor Space: **65,000 square feet**. Number of Levels: **1**. Contract Cost: **US$7 million**. Completed: **March 1998**.

opposite Section through the 11th-floor of the New York Port Authority Building.
above The sparse and robust open work setting.

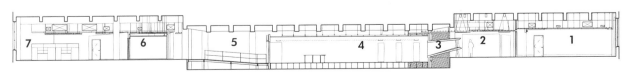

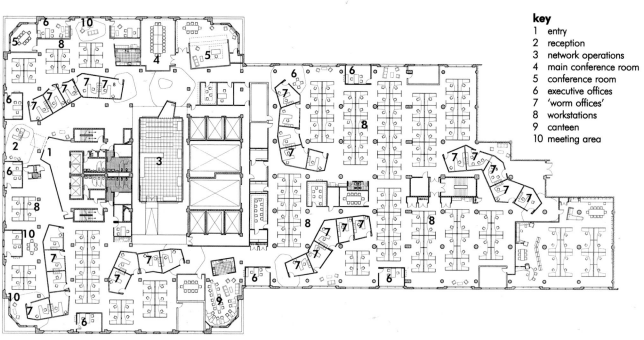

key
1 entry
2 reception
3 network operations
4 main conference room
5 conference room
6 executive offices
7 'worm offices'
8 workstations
9 canteen
10 meeting area

opposite above Reception area.
opposite below The floor plan shows the worm-like management office enclosures which slither between structural columns.
right A manager's enclosed office.
below The perimeter canteen.

When an interior design company decides to move to a new studio space, its workplace is immediately judged as a test of its standards as a practice. So it helps if (a) the building has a strong character from which the interior scheme can develop; and (b) the budget is large enough to do the conversion in style. But in the case of the relocation of Madrid design firm Empty to converted commercial premises in the city's Calle Linneo, these advantages were distinctly lacking. The building was mediocre, hemmed in by other commercial property with only one narrow external access, and the budget was tight.

Rather than 'dress' the interior, architect Victor López Cotelo decided to strip it back to the essentials to reveal a simple, spacious structure with industrial finishes that make a virtue out of their modesty. False ceilings were ripped out and several skylights inserted to bring natural light into double-height workspaces which were formerly cramped and poorly lit. Soft blinds prevent the sunlight becoming too intrusive. Flexibility, order and light were the architect's watchwords. The scheme arranges individual offices with translucent glass partitions, administrative areas and washrooms around a

large, open-plan area, taking advantage of the double-height space to insert a mezzanine work level.

The fittings and furnishings were created by one of Empty's own designers, Luis Díaz Mauriño, with Empty director Francisco Mínguez Coll. The desks, for example, are made of bevelled birch with galvanized steel legs, while birch shelving differentiates key areas. Wooden panels and a white-painted tubular metal glazing system stand out among the spare componetry of the project.

Rietveld drawings, Le Corbusier sofas and an Alto chaise longue exist amid an otherwise plain treatment. But it is Victor López Cotelo's refusal to decorate that gives the Empty studio its composure. He concentrates instead on structure, form, materials and dimensions – what he describes as 'the relationship between large and small, near and distant, open and closed' – to pleasing effect.

Designer: **Victor López Cotelo**. Commissioning Client: **Francisco Mínguez Coll, Empty**. Total Floor Space: **700 square metres**. Number of Levels: **1**. Contract Cost: **£115,000**. Completed: **December 1998**.

left and opposite Interior views reveal a stripped-back aesthetic and custom joinery.
below Floor plan.

key (below)
1 existing building
2 garage
3 foyer
4 open office
5 meeting room

key (right)
1 open office
2 offices
3 management
4 meeting room
5 canteen
6 patio

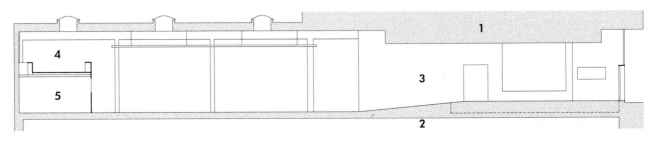

When Mexican cement producer Cemex commissioned British architects Nicholas Grimshaw & Partners to design a new computer centre to manage its global production, stock and distribution round the clock, 365 days a year, total security was a priority. So was a high degree of environmental control, given the Mexican climate. But this project is no forbidding high-tech bunker. Its futuristic interior projects a dynamic company identity, reflecting the ingenuity with which its designers have turned constraints into opportunities.

A key to the approach is the use of two different lighting scenarios: one for everyday and one for special VIP visits. Lighting designer on the project was Jonathan Speirs. Visitors experience the different spaces of the building as though passing through Stanley Kubrick-inspired film sets. The sequence starts as visitors negotiate a special security lock before entering the centre. This in itself is dramatic: a heavy, stainless-steel door slides back to usher visitors into a small, enclosed space lit only by blue indirect lighting in the perforations of the door. Red globes recessed into the ceiling then give the impression of 'scanning' the visitor. Finally, only when the sliding door is completely closed, a second set of doors open to reveal the computer centre.

This environment expresses the idea of climate control with an 'ice house' aesthetic. Etched glass lenses that emit blue light are set in a raised floor covered with patterned stainless steel. Four etched glass cutouts reveal thousands of cables acting as the nerves of the computer centre. The control desk overlooks the whole operation from an elliptical platform separated only by a full-height glass screen. Staff here work on a carpeted island below a highly translucent textile ceiling that provides warm, indirect light. Client presentations can be projected on to a white, tensioned sail suspended from the concrete slab end wall opposite the control desk. Whoever said computer centres were boring?

Architect: **Nicholas Grimshaw & Partners**.
Commissioning Client: **Cemex**. Total Floor Space:**1,200 square metres**. Number of Levels: **1**. Contract Cost: **US$1.1 million**. Completed: **September 1997**.

opposite Red ceiling globes 'scan' visitors in the security-lock entrance to the Mexican computer centre.
below The floor plan reveals the dominance of the control desk on the stainless-steel grid.

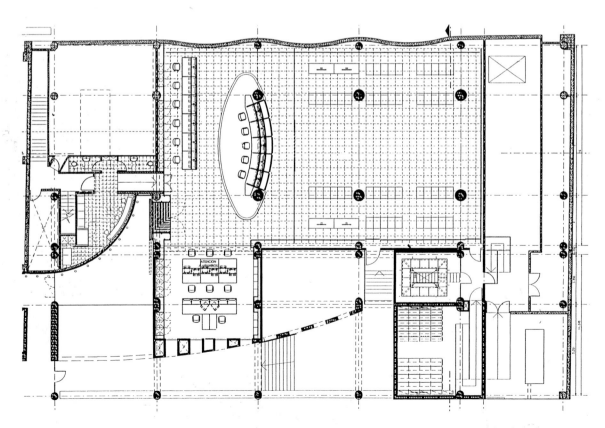

above and right The 'James Bond' image of the climate-controlled centre is expressed using etched glass, recessed lights and overt displays of technology.

In some ways this project, on a prime riverbank site north of the Thames between Westminster and Blackfriars, is a throwback to the days of the monolithic workplace: a grand global headquarters with a great deal of cellular office space and bland air of discreet corporate professionalism. But look beyond the restraint of the sober eight-storey glass and stone façade and the formality of the floor plans, and you will find aspects of this scheme that are novel. In an age when open plan is orthodox, the decision to line the perimeter with glass-walled cellular workspaces of assorted sizes is reformist in character. It takes the 'hoteling' idea of office space to a new level of sophistication, using a customized glazing system and an adaptation of Unifor's Italian modular furniture subtly to create effective private but 'open' workspaces.

Globe House, as British American Tobacco's new home is called, accommodates 650 people in conditions of relative spaciousness. The building was developed speculatively, but a GMW design team led by John Bevan has been careful to give it a de luxe fit-out tailored precisely to client needs. On every level of the project, which is dominated by a soaring limestone-floored central atrium and crowned by a smart eighth-floor mezzanine entertaining suite with great river views, there is a sense of quiet confidence.

A specially commissioned entrance mural and reception desk of glass, steel and stone set the tone. Thereafter, the main points of visual interest are activity rooms off the main stairway that showcase company events and initiatives. A Lucky Strike diner, for example, dressed with gaudy chrome, illustrates a café concept that the company is planning to franchise around the world to promote its famous brand. A large and impressive restaurant, video-conferencing suites and private dining areas, meeting and internet-surfing complete 'an office for living in', as John Bevan describes it.

Designer: **GMW Partnership**. Commissioning Client: **British American Tobacco**. Total Floor Space: **25,398 square metres**. Number of Levels: **10**. Contract Cost: **£32 million**. Completed: **December 1998**.

top The ground-floor plan shows the extent of the public, restaurant and meeting facilities.
above A typical office-floor plan shows the high degree of perimeter cellular officing.
opposite A view of the limestone-floored central atrium around which facilities are grouped.

opposite A private executive dining suite with roof terrace offers spectacular views over the River Thames. **above** The custom glazing system creates cellular offices while maintaining an open feel to the environment. Furniture is by the Italian company Unifor. **left** Artwork enlivens the restaurant.

The New Jersey headquarters of healthcare advertising agency Torre Lazur offers a pleasant suburban site and an easy commute for most of its employees. But for the copywriters and art directors of its creative department, what was missing was any real sense of Manhattan buzz. Not only that, conditions were overcrowded and the agency was unable to boast about its investment in creative talent to prospective clients. This project by architects Lazslo Kiss and Todd Zwigard gives 135 Torre Lazur creative staff their own workspace on one floor which recreates the pulse and edginess of New York City in its form and materials, and provides a showcase for visitors from the medical industry.

The scheme draws heavily on Kiss + Zwigard's experience in exhibition design. Space is arranged around a promenade, or 'main street', which zig-zags through the creative area, taking clients and visitors on a tour of facilities. Elevated six inches above surrounding offices, this promenade is designed with a curving rubber floor and sloping walls on a metal-stud skeleton to create the effect of being on a ship. The walls are made of marker board, which can be written or drawn on freely and then erased. The promenade, which varies in width from eight to twelve feet, is not simply a circulation route; it acts as a multi-functional space for client presentations, brainstorms, parties and other activities. Impromptu meetings are encouraged to stimulate the flow of creative ideas.

There is a sense of things happening wherever you look. Portals leading to the four main departments – copy,

art, studio and traffic – have been cut into the promenade. These departments occupy the four quadrants of the floor plate and are defined by different-coloured carpet-tile patterns. A waiting and gathering area, which prefaces the promenade, has large windows punched into its walls to afford glimpses of the inner workings of the agency. Around the perimeter of this level, private offices are organized against a translucent screen wall that allows exterior light to penetrate deep into the interior from the south, west and north sides. Torre Lazur wants to attract more cutting-edge talent to its business. This creative vessel is enough to make even the most hip art director forget about the downside of coming to work each day in Parsipanny, New Jersey.

Designers: **Kiss + Zwigard Architects**. Commissioning Client: **Torre Lazur Communication**. Total Floor Space: **25,000 square feet**. Number of Levels: **1**. Contract Cost: **Confidential**. Completed: **October 1997**.

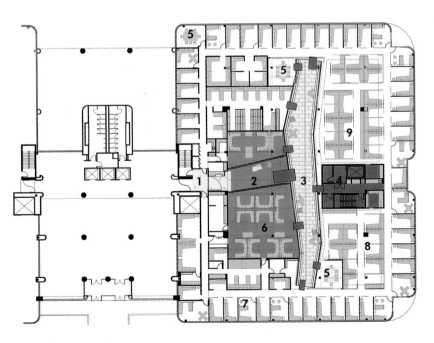

key
1 vestibule
2 waiting area
3 promenade
4 kitchen
5 meeting rooms
6 computer studio
7 production area
8 art department
9 copy

above Ship-like metal cladding and exposed services bring an urban edginess to this suburban workplace.
opposite The floor plan shows the central promenade which cuts through the creative area, and an exploded section reveals its curved complexity.

below The view along the elevated central promenade, a multi-functional creative space for impromptu meetings and events.
opposite An open work area. Translucent materials are designed to support team working.

Some of the most radical examples of new work patterns within organizations can be found in unremarkable and drab interiors. At the other extreme, there are visually exciting and advanced office environments which incongruously accommodate a traditional work process. This project for Dutch insurance company Interpolis is different and special because it does a rare thing: it combines genuinely new ways of working, based on innovative technologies, with office interiors that exude creative quality and intelligent thinking at every turn.

The Interpolis building, close to Tilburg's business district, attaches a low-rise annexe with a spectacular entrance hall to a thin tower which provides 20 intimate office floors for team-working. These have small floor plates and a high degree of flexibility, due to the use of moveable partitions. The public elements of the facility – the entrance hall, with its bold perforated metal units and information pillars, restaurant and sculpture garden – dramatically illustrate the Interpolis philosophy that 'your place of work is wherever you happen to be'. Cordless telephone, networked laptop and computer-based intranet systems allow staff to roam the building, work where they want and track the movements of visitors without unsightly wires or Post-it notes.

At the entrance to each team floor in the tower, employees check their pigeonhole, pick up their cordless phone and collect their 'flexi-case' containing their personal effects. They then either select to work in a private 'cockpit' or in one of a number of informal open areas, which have glazed partitions and natural wood finishes that create a calm environment. To avoid uniformity in the high rise, each team floor is prefaced by a lively café themed around a different world city. Choices range from Rio to Barcelona; but judging by the success of this scheme – Interpolis has achieved 30 per cent savings on its property costs – the place to be is Tilburg.

Architect: **Abe Bonnema (Bureau for Architecture and Environmental Planning)**. Interior Designer: **Kho Liang le Associates**. Commissioning Client: **Interpolis**. Total Floor Space: **125,000 square feet**. Number of Levels: **20**. Contract Cost: **£56 million**. Completed: **November 1997**.

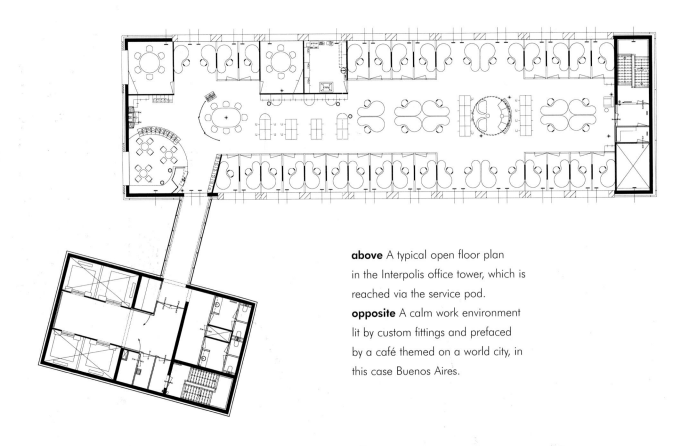

above A typical open floor plan in the Interpolis office tower, which is reached via the service pod.
opposite A calm work environment lit by custom fittings and prefaced by a café themed on a world city, in this case Buenos Aires.

left and below The bold main entrance hall provides a setting for mobile work amid perforated and wave-form elements in metal.

2 leisure

leisure projects

2.3

2.9

Life is a curved wall glimpsed through a porthole for the designer of contemporary leisure interiors.

Fun is rubberized and cartoonlike for kids, style-conscious and calmly sophisticated for adults.

From cotton, linen and coloured glass to rolled steel and plywood stools, tactile materials are enriching the user experience.

Health and fitness is communicated everywhere by pools of blue light, luminous surfaces and gleaming finishes.

Abstract impression is in. Literal representation is out: the shimmering silver cone, not the spaceship.

Brown lignite bricks are stacked to suggest a book-lined basement club, steel ceiling girders evoke a leafy forest in a health spa.

Hotel conversions appeal to former golden ages – the New York of the 1930s, the Copenhagen of Arne Jacobsen in the 1950s.

Adventurous spatial concepts are implemented despite the constraints of historic buildings.

2.10

2.1 one aldwych london, uk

Once the Edwardian offices of the *Morning Post* newspaper, One Aldwych has been transformed by architects Jestico + Whiles into a prestigious hotel with a dazzling lobby and bar. The client, hotelier Gordon Campbell Gray, brought a distinctive personal approach to the project based on his own mistrust of the dreary 'de luxe' hotel features he encountered while travelling; Gray wanted One Aldwych to display above all a classic feel rather than superficial 'designer' credentials.

One Aldwych is a distinguished building on a triangular island site at the meeting point of the City of London and the West End. The original 1906 structure was one of the first in London to use the American 'Columbian' construction system of a steel frame with reinforced concrete floors. With its 1920s extension of two upper floors, One Aldwych is now a Grade II-listed building and in addition to the usual concerns of preservation, the conversion from offices to hotel prompted three major design decisions. The first was to transform the existing double-height lobby into a high-impact focal point for the hotel. The second was to install an innovative vacuum-powered drainage system to do away with conventional service ducts that would have cluttered precious ground-floor space. The third was to expand the mean central staircase into a more celebratory circulation route by creating an open lobby on each floor and a new, wider stone stair which is ingeniously threaded through the building.

The effect was to open up the building's interior, replacing the functional lineaments of office circulation with the more theatrical experience demanded by a hotel that also features a basement health club in which the musculature of original studded steel columns is artfully exposed. In total, 106 rooms and suites are located on six floors within the building's irregular steel skeleton. When the novelty of the theatrical lobby wears off, it seems more than likely that the thoughtfulness of Jestico + Whiles' systemic conversion will ensure the classic status the client sought is maintained. Architect: **Jestico + Whiles Architects**. Interior Planning: **Jestico +Whiles Interiors**. Commissioning Client: **One Aldwych/Gordon Campbell Gray** .Total Floor Space: **100,000 square feet**. Number of Levels: **6**. Contract Cost: **£20 million**. Completed: **July 1998**.

right A handsome grand lobby forms the heart of the hotel project.
above right The exploded axonometric reveals the plan for a building that was a pioneer of new construction techniques in 1906.

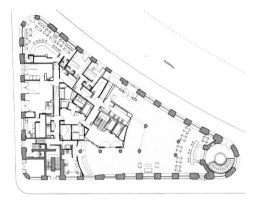

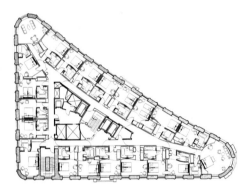

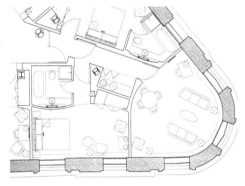

above The ground-floor and first-floor plans
and typical suite layout.
right The hotel swimming pool in the
basement health club with steel columns
of the building's original structure exposed
to give an appropriately muscular feel.

This minimalist eaterie, inserted with consummate skill into the former stables of a Renaissance structure which has been the seat of provincial government in Graz since the mid-sixteenth century, has a certain historical inevitability about it. The original architect of the three-storey building, constructed between 1557 and 1565, was an Italian, Domenico Allio. So is the designer of the new Johan restaurant, London-based Claudio Silvestrin. The work of the former has been meticulously respected by the latter, not only because of the insistence of the Historic Landmarks Commission that the original space be preserved but also because local sensibilities are at stake. Turning a section of the Landhaus, part of the regional political fabric, into yet another venue for the fashionable dining set was always likely to be frowned upon in some quarters.

As an interior designer, however, Silvestrin can be relied upon not to scare the horses. Everything he does is measured and calm, logical and graceful. The restaurant entrance is the soul of discretion, retaining the original dark slate pavings from the sixteenth-century stables. Inside, a barrel-vaulted anteroom surfaced in beige Italian sandstone tiling features long walls lined with low-backed teak benches with canvas-covered cushions, teak-topped tables and laminated plywood stools. Through the low light of single white candles one can discern a massive entrance at the far end of the anteroom which leads to the restaurant itself.

Beneath a limewashed ceiling, which is supported by stone columns and expressed as a succession of rhythmic gothic arches, this main restaurant space is knowingly sparse and sculptural. Parallel rows of simply dressed tables are matched by functionalist 1920s furniture in a setting that avoids an all-controlling coldness by use of eye-level square mirrors and concealed heating units in the floor and walls. Glass panes fixed in pairs of windows situated in each arch are artificially lit to cast a greyish-white glow in daytime and an otherworldy blue at night. Two curved plaster walls, designed to 'float' and pigment-coloured to match 'the grey velour of high heel shoes', according to the client, conceal the kitchen – the final flourish in a scheme of great finesse.

Architect: **Claudio Silvestrin**. Commissioning Client: **Elke Osthus and Heinz Steinberger**. Total Floor Space: **250 square metres**. Number of Levels: **1**. Contract Cost: **Confidential**. Completed: **Autumn 1997**.

below The floor plan shows the anteroom that serves as a prelude to the main restaurant interior.
opposite Gracefully lit gothic arches punctuate a sparse and sculptural main eating area.
overleaf The barrel-vaulted anteroom, bar area and entrance to the Johan restaurant.

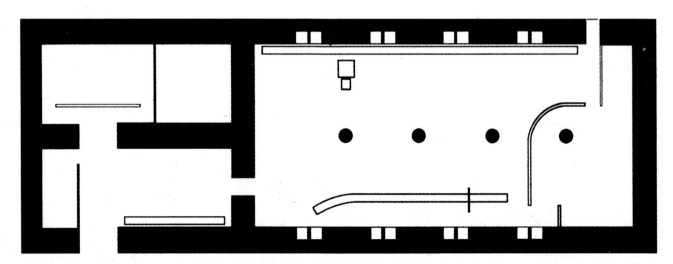

A frighteningly short, 12-week, construction schedule seems somehow appropriate to a corner-site Chinese restaurant that incorporates a fast takeout service as an adjunct to its striking interior. But no matter how impatient the young graduates of the Mackintosh School of Architecture in Glasgow who make up Studio MG are for success and recognition, it must have been a strain to achieve. Yet Yeung's fairly fizzes with design innovation and a kind of joyful urgency.

The corner site allows fully glazed visibility of an interior dominated by brushed zinc. The innovative flooring is composed of white, poured latex that gives a seamless finish and makes it one of the few uninterrupted planes in the whole interior. Even so, there are three levels and many disjointed partitions, walls and panels to make Yeung's look busy even when it is empty. The effect is calculated, drawing together proprietor Joseph Ngan's commercial concerns to eliminate the yawning spaces that deter customers from coming in with Studio MG's own fondness for broken sightlines and fractured shapes.

Surprising details abound, such as the angular 'shadows' of the zinc handrails, columns and bar which have been painted on to the white floor. The designers' own paintings appear on the walls and an oblique panel of tropical olive wood with Italian polished plaster adds a more traditional notion of 'quality'. Arne Jacobsen chairs are disposed around the tables in quartets, but with three white ones for each black. The white chairs 'disappear' against the white floor, just as each black one stands out.

If the initial visual effect of Yeung's is one of controlled subsidence, Studio MG is happy. Upsetting familiar expectations is something it enjoys doing. Its plan was to reinvent the concept of a traditional Cantonese restaurant, and in the process reposition it for a 24-hour culture that suits the location. Yeung's is no cosy retreat for a traditional Chinese lunch or evening meal. Rather, it is a continually accessible dining resource combining food, bar drinks and takeout waiting area within the confines of a lively spatial and visual adventure. Architect: **Studio MG**. Commissioning Client: **Rocheway Ltd**. Total Floor Space: **456 square metres**. Number of Levels: **1**. Contract Cost: **£200,000**. Completed: **January 1999**.

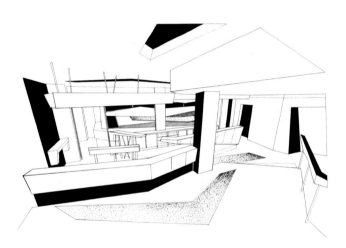

above and below The exploded view and sections reveal the spatial ambition and angular character of the project.
opposite The main bar area. Broken and interrupted sightlines across a plain of seamless latex flooring makes the place look busy even when it is empty.

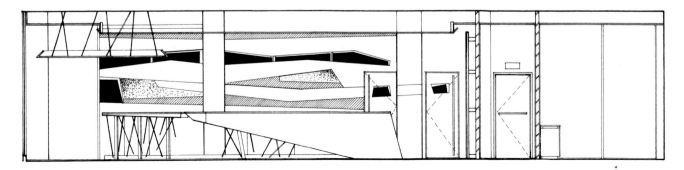

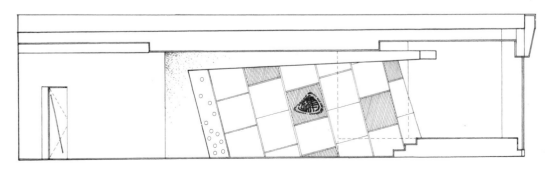

left The main eating area with its diagonal axis. Idiosyncratic railings and light totems frame the formal simplicity of the setting. **below** Angled panels of tropical olive wood set off by a strip of polished Italian plaster reveal attention to detail every bit as expansive as the grand plan.

The Roger Williams is not alone among old Manhattan hotels that have outlived their early 1930s glory. By the early 1990s it had, however, sunk to an exceptional low. Then the Gotham Hospitality Group's Bernard Goldberg decided that the building met his criterion of being 'a property with real value' to which more value could be added. Goldberg had already worked the trick with other Manhattan hotels – The Wales, The Franklin, The Mansfield and The Shoreham – but the 207-room Roger Williams was to be the first such venture using New York architect Rafael Viñoly, best known for his stunning glass Tokyo International Forum.

Located on Madison Avenue in Manhattan's garment district, the Roger Williams needed to maintain its high room count to be viable, and the renovation budget was not high. Viñoly responded to a property he called 'a disaster' with a multi-pronged strategy that tied the building into the street line, sacrificed a few second-floor rooms to create a more impressive lobby and then went to considerable lengths to make the guest rooms look small by choice rather than out of necessity. At street level, the hotel's new façade borrowed the limestone of an adjacent church. Above, the existing brick has been cleaned and repointed while the roofline is newly articulated with evergreen trees. The revamped, 20-foot-high lobby with its zinc-clad columns, maple panelling, Tibetan carpet and vintage Steinway, opens on to the street with full-height windows and a canopied main entrance on Madison Avenue. Reconfiguration of the upper rooms and services was necessarily restricted to fine tuning, but the rooms themselves feature Viñoly-designed furniture and accessories as well as glass bathroom partitions, blue limestone tiles and slate countertops.

The architect's earlier work on the Tokyo International Forum may have something to do with a scheme that manages to infuse small spaces with a feeling of considerable quality. This effect is achieved by a shrewd choice of materials that will be touched (for example, the cedar shower floor grilles and quality cotton linen) rather than miniaturized clichés of opulence.

Designer: **Rafael Viñoly**. Commissioning Client: **The Gotham Hospitality Group**. Total Floor Space: **100,000 square feet**. Number of Levels: **14**. Contract Cost: **US$10 million**. Completed: **Autumn 1997**.

left One of Manhattan's finest hotels of the 1930s expertly restored.
opposite The refurbished lobby with its fluted, zinc-clad columns and classic grand piano.
below The first-floor plan.

key
1 entry
2 main lobby
3 sculpture lounge
4 reception lobby
5 reception desk
6 office

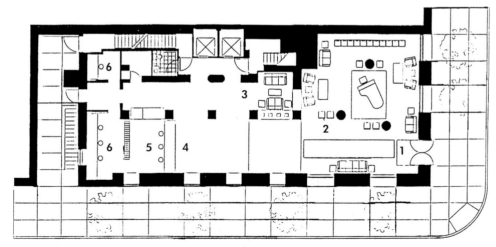

opposite Views towards the main lobby area and of the main entrance suggest the conscious evocation of former greatness. Wheeler Williams' 1934 sculpture *The Four Seasons* keeps a watchful eye.

above A guestroom fitted with an ensemble of maple veneer furnishings. Small dimensions are turned to advantage through intimacy of scale and simple detailing.

This scheme to create a substantial new facility that would expand spa tourism in the small German village of Bad Colberg, where thermal springs were first discovered in the early years of the twentieth century, was always going to be controversial. Critics who pointed out the potential adverse effects on the local landscape were opposed by those who argued in favour of the economic benefits the new complex would bring. It was left to architects Kauffmann Theilig & Partner to reconcile opposing views by designing a new state-of-the-art clinic and spa that would merge with the sloping landscape. The resulting scheme, which splits the programme into several low-lying buildings covered with landscaped roof meadows and gravel borders to improve environmental integration in a sequence of terraces, not only achieves that primary aim but also creates several impressive interior spaces.

Bad Colberg's original horseshoe-shaped arrangement of spa buildings, built in Art Nouveau style, were opened in 1910. Sited in the region of Thuringen, they became a retreat for privileged party officials during the era of the German Democratic Republic. Following reunification, the regional authorities debated how to upgrade a neglected spa clinic where time had stood still. The architects have been uncompromisingly modern in their approach. The new-build scheme links a flexibly divided therapy centre, which includes a dining hall, kitchen and service rooms, to a series of four hotel-style patient blocks grouped around an inner space; these four 'houses' contain a total of 300 patient rooms among them. The use of floor-to-ceiling glass walls and an absence of pediments and hard borders emphasizes the link to the local landscape.

The thermal bath itself is housed in a separate building at the south-east of the site which presents a 'cascade' of 11 differently sized round basins ranged over several levels within a 'bathing landscape'. These sit beneath a sloping, lightweight steel-and-glass roof featuring a pattern of steel girders that is reminiscent of leaves. The designers avoided conventional coloured or glazed bath ceramics, specifying instead stone-grey tiles which provide a smooth transition between the internal and external environment. Lighting integrated into the basins creates glowing pools at night, but during the day the effect is of bathing outside.

Architect: **Kauffmann Theilig & Partner**. Commissioning Client: **Bad Colberg Kliniken**. Total Floor Space per storey: **22,883 square metres** (split into: patient houses, 10,535 square metres; therapy, 8,115 square metres; health spa, 4,233 square metres; pool area, 600 square metres). Contract Cost: **DM 100 million**. Completed: **April 1997**.

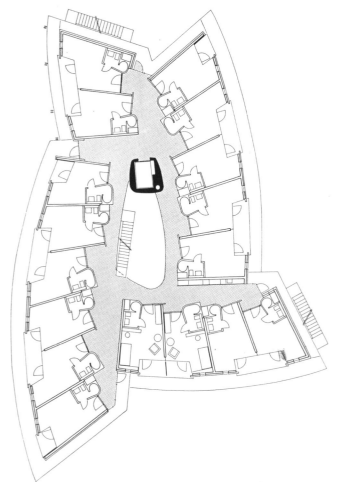

left A typical floor plan for a patient block.
opposite The thermal bath area with its sloping, glass-and-steel roof designed to express the idea of looking up through a canopy of trees.

left Wooden slats and stone-grey tiles are incorporated into the pool area to harmonize the interior with the natural environment outside.

below Section through the entire facility, which sits in the sloping landscape.

bottom The 'cascade' of bathing basins (left) and an exploded diagram showing the layers of the thermal bath ceiling construction (right).

opposite Sails and stairs form a colourful and engaging configuration in one of the main clinics.

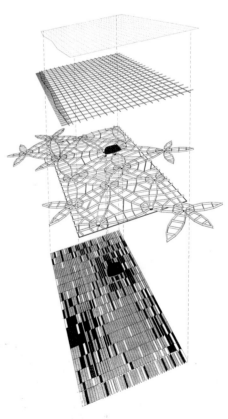

2.6 `time beach bar` whitley bay, uk

Whitley Bay is the type of traditional seaside resort in the north-east of England you see featured in old sepia post-cards. The Time Beach Bar (sometimes referred to as the Time 'Intergalactic' Beach Bar by its designer Paul Daly) looks as if it has arrived there from outer space, or at least from Hollywood. Into the routine seaside townscape of Whitley Bay's pubs and bingo halls (and specifically into the very traditional Rex Hotel on the promenade) has come a luminous bar suggesting alien intrusion rather than any logical extension of the hotel's character. Of course, that was the idea. Daly's intention was to create something so much more dramatic than the local competition that the only failure would have been not to go over the top.

Disks, saucers and portholes form the recurring motifs in a sinuously electric environment calculated to make an impression. The ceiling is animated with cut-out circles. A 'chromawall' with constantly changing coloured squares casts a variable eerie glow. Features include portholes and mirrors, elliptical seating and tables, serpentine bar fronts and various versions of Daly's signature shape, a square with rounded corners. Slatted blinds offer a fretted view of Whitley Bay by day and shut it out at night. A variety of flooring materials and raised sections at either end of the venue add spatial texture. One of the raised sections is a dance floor, the other a seating area. Detail and visual impact aside, there is a very logical flow to the club interior and this is extended by a long corridor lined with vertical mirrors (again in Daly's signature lozenge shape) set against a purple wall. The corridor leads to the toilets and, eventually, to the earthbound interior of the Rex Hotel. Daly – who is inclined to statements like, 'Sometimes it is design's destiny to seek out new worlds and boldly go where no designer has gone before' – has found in client Ultimate Leisure a kindred spirit dedicated to enlivening the low-key leisure haunts of England's north-east coastline with design that would not look out of place in New York or Barcelona ... or Mars.

Designer: **Paul Daly Design Studio**. Commissioning Client: **Ultimate Leisure**. Total Floor Space: **2,000 square feet**. Number of Levels: **1**. Contract Cost: **£500,000**. Completed: **Winter 1998**.

right Disks, saucers, portholes and cut-out circles dominate but the designer's signature shape is the oblong or rounded square.

opposite and this page
Interior views of the
Time Beach Bar reveal
Daly's controlled
energy in using custom
furniture and lighting
design to create a highly
individual environment.

This project to upgrade the guest bedrooms and bathrooms of Arne Jacobsen's classic 1959 SAS Royal Hotel opposite the Tivoli Gardens in Copenhagen brings a refreshing contemporary touch to one of the most sacred icons of Scandinavian modernism. Jacobsen (1902–71) is still rightly revered in his homeland and much of his work, especially his furniture, remains commercially and artistically relevant. But hotel interiors always need to move on, and Yasmine Mahmoudieh has not shirked this sensitive task. The resulting scheme pays homage to Jacobsen and the golden post-war age of Danish design in its forms and materials but is inescapably of today.

The horizontal stripes on the façade of Jacobsen's unusually brutal hotel block are reflected in the interiors. But it is another repeated design – the 'kidney' shape made popular in the 1950s – that gives the five-star guest bedrooms their distinctive personality. This motif is manifested in lighting fixtures set within curved wooden walls behind the beds, in contrasting-coloured ovals in the carpeting and in sandblasted glass elements in the cabinet-mirrors. The palette of materials is typically Danish: maple wood, coloured glass, aluminium and local fabrics. The three different colour schemes for the suites – yellow-beige in combination with green, red or blue – relate to the verdigris roofs, red brick buildings and blue skies that can be seen from the hotel's upper floors.

The rooms are lit by a combination of indirect lighting, to create atmosphere, and direct task lighting, to enable guests to read and work comfortably at the desk or in bed. Much of the lighting is skilfully integrated into furniture. Rigorous attention to detail extends to the renovated bathrooms, which repeat the hotel's horizontal grid in their blue and green tiling and include the maple wood and coloured glass elements of the bedrooms. Arne Jacobsen was renowned for making functionalism beautiful and comfortable. This update is very much in his spirit.

Designer: **Mahmoudieh Design**. Commissioning Client: **Radisson SAS**. Total Floor Space: **10,400 square metres.** Number of Rooms: **260**. Contract Cost: **40 million Danish Crowns**. Completed: **June 1999**.

opposite The refurbished guest bedrooms and bathrooms use a typically Danish palette of materials and the kidney-shaped motif of the 1950s in delicate homage to architect Arne Jacobsen.
below Typical layout of the guestrooms in the classic 1959 hotel.

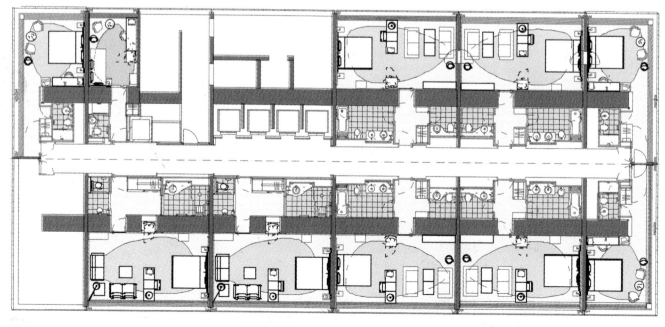

This luminous health club facility was conceived as a sister enterprise to the Broadgate Club, opened in 1989 as part of the City of London's Broadgate development. The new club, located on the northern borders of London's West End, is also part of a major development, British Land's Regent's Place, designed by Arup Associates. Intended by the client to be a cutting-edge example for the health and fitness industry, Broadgate Club West is situated within the ground floor of the Triton Square Building.

Where the original Broadgate club enjoyed the high quality surroundings of its famous City development, the new club in Regent's Place is rather more stranded, part of a smaller island in a less affluent urban setting close to Euston Station. In response, architects Allford Hall Monaghan Morris took the boldest of approaches to the interior design, creating an environment that is simultaneously practical and fantastical. Broadgate West is all gleaming drama with translucent partitions, flowing colour, nautical imagery and luxurious finishes, as well as changing coloured lights that suffuse walls at the touch of a switch. The main visual feature is a glazed, backlit blue wall inspired by a blue tile mural by Howard Hodgkin in the City club. This winds from the building's entrance façade through the full length of the club, a luminous thread tying everything together.

The blue wall typifies the club's playfulness with light and materials. It is created by backlighting laminate glass with an opalescent interlayer, a system that proved the most efficient at diffusing light. Light fittings are installed on the plasterboard wall that forms the back face of the lighting access corridor. Cold cathode technology ensures low heat output and economical running costs and enables a programmable system that controls dimming and can create fades, flash sequences and gradual blends. Graphics and signage by Studio Myerscough, which help to define the club's various zones and facilities, even include the odd haiku on the wall.

Designer: **Allford Hall Monaghan Morris Architects**.
Commissioning Client: **The Broadgate Club**. Total Floor Space: **2,020 square metres**. Number of Levels: **1**.
Contract Cost: **£2.5 million**. Completed: **December 1997**.

opposite Fitness machines adopt anthropomorphic identities.
below Ground-floor plan.

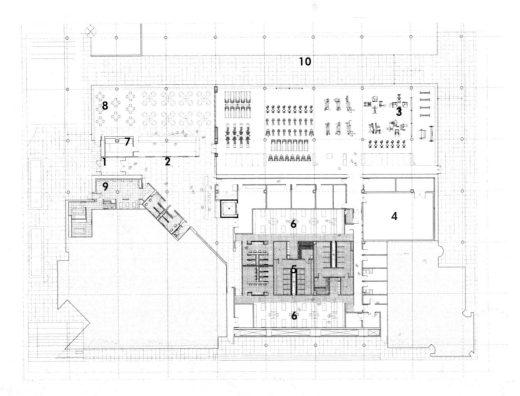

key
1 entrance hall
2 lobby
3 gymnasium
4 dance studio
5 shower and saunas
6 changing rooms
7 bar
8 lounge
9 hair salon
10 arcade

below Colour-coded graphics by Studio Myerscough direct newcomers to the right equipment.
right The 'blue wall' visual feature is created by back-lighting laminate glass with an opalescent interlayer.

opposite The stylish bar area, which is connected to reception by a single, slatted wall.
above Changing rooms are on either side of a blue-tiled wet area.

Faced with a restaurant client who is not only a gourmet but an art collector, architects von Gerkan Marg did an eminently sensible thing: they developed a scheme that turns the white stucco walls of this Berlin eaterie into a prominent and well-lit venue for changing contemporary art exhibitions. The setting for Restaurant Vau is a late-nineteenth-century building close to the Gendermenmarkt in the centre of the city, but nothing remained of the original interior fittings to give the project its creative cue.

Instead the designers opted for what they describe as 'congenial modern comfort'. Diners enter Restaurant Vau via a brightly lit route that leads to an inner courtyard. To the right of the entrance is a salon finished in red Venetian stucco and divided off for private functions from the main restaurant area by room-height sliding doors. To the left is the main restaurant space, featuring a dark, American walnut floor and a barrel-vaulted ceiling lined with perforated Swiss pearwood. The art sits on white walls articulated with recesses into which

black leather benches have been fitted. A staircase, also surfaced in dark American walnut, leads down to a bar beneath the courtyard where the whiff of exclusivity of the more formal restaurant gives way to the casual, intimate atmosphere of a cellar bar.

The downstairs bar area also boasts one of the scheme's truly original interior flourishes – one and a half tons of East German brown lignite bricks, stacked like books in small illuminated wooden compartments. It is both a reminder that the location once housed the largest private coal store in the world, and a flash of inspiration. The feel is of a library or club given contemporary industrial expression with the use of complementary slate paving and high drinks tables covered in rolled steel.

Architect: **gmp (von Gerkan Marg and Partner).**
Commissioning Client: **Gregor Hoheisel**. Total Floor Space: **170 square metres.** Number of Levels: **1**. Contract Cost: **DM 1.8 million**. Completed: **February 1997**.

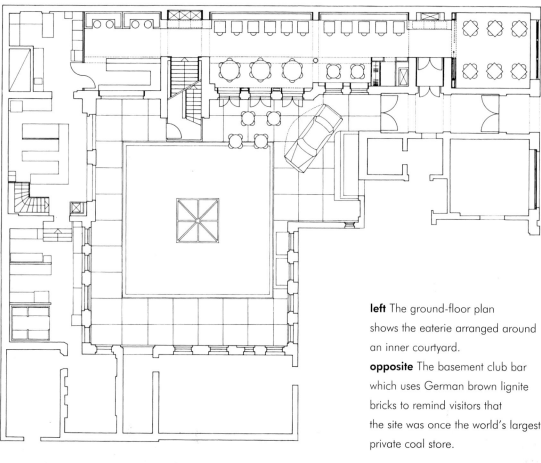

left The ground-floor plan shows the eaterie arranged around an inner courtyard.
opposite The basement club bar which uses German brown lignite bricks to remind visitors that the site was once the world's largest private coal store.

above The brown bricks stacked like books give the interior the calm authority of a library or study.

opposite and above right The main ground-floor restaurant with its barrel-vaulted ceiling lined with Swiss pearwood. This thin, gallery-like space is ideal for displaying artworks.

This prototypical activity centre is a larger version of a facility which Bright Child has run for the past decade, offering an imaginative, secure and engaging environment for children of various ages. The principles were already broadly established (high security and safety, non-literal features, no straight walls) and Kanner Architects, working with associate architect Michael Kovac, were retained to inject fun and whimsy into a project with a budget of only $30 per square foot. The location is a highly visible space on Fourth Street in the heart of Santa Monica's revitalized downtown area.

Keeping children safe within the confines of Bright Child's premises was a high priority for the client so computer bracelets are used to monitor where they are, preventing unauthorized departure. The interior is characterized by soft, curving walls, rubber bumper cushions on all square edges and flooring that is either carpeted or rubberized. The activity centre aims to appeal to both children and parents, and Kanner Architects' reputation in pop architecture ensured shapes and features that would amuse adults and engage children. Making a virtue out of a budgetary necessity, Kanner eschewed literal representation and detailed features

in favour of treatments that simply suggest a variety of textures and materials. In this way a 'thatched bamboo' hut is recreated using a set of intersecting wooden cubes. Meanwhile, a spaceship is represented by a silver shimmering cone with pink interior walls. The client can therefore claim a strategy that stimulates the child's imagination, while the architect can use relatively inexpensive materials to create simple but witty 3-D icons.

The activities within Bright Child range from arts and crafts and computer classes to sports and birthday party events, and there is a dedicated space for infants and toddlers. Bright Child also accommodates one of America's largest and most complex tubular play structures. However, perhaps the strongest impact comes from Kanner's bold disposition of spaces and coloured finishes – all oblique windows, vibrant hues, giant peepholes and the spatial logic of a bright cartoon made real.

Designer: **Kanner Architects.** Commissioning Client: **Bright Child**. Total Floor Space: **8,000 square feet.** Number of Levels: **1**. Contract Cost: **$240,000**. Completed: **September 1998**.

key
1 reception
2 corridoor
3 large play area
4 mini play area
5 basketball court
6 party rooms
7 lunch area
8 arts and crafts
9 bath areas

opposite and overleaf The jaunty angles, suggestive shapes and rubberized forms of Bright Child are designed to stimulate the imagination while ensuring safety.

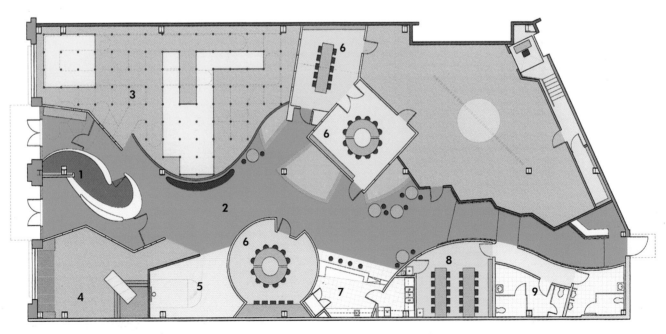

above The café area aims
to make the facility appeal
to adults as well as kids.
left Abstract icons leave
it to young users to apply
a meaning.
opposite The designers
complied with the client's
demand for 'no straight walls',
as this party setting shows.

In a small Sardinian seaside resort, a client found himself in possession of a redundant 1970s discothèque that had not aged well. Unmatched to contemporary tourist tastes both by dated design and a basement location, the premises needed to be reinvented as a leisure attraction for holidaymakers more accustomed to open-air bars and cafés. Architect Pierluigi Piu had to address both of these problems, as well as the client's stated preference for using a metal sheeting as part of the design solution; the client's main business being the sale and working of metal sheeting.

Out of this highly pragmatic brief, Piu has created a subterranean piano bar that makes a triumphant virtue out of all of its restrictions. Taking a submarine theme (to make the basement location seem logical rather than inappropriate), Piu employs distressed metal features, subtle naval imagery, exposed bolts and myriad other effects all aimed at giving the visitor a sense of 'immersion' in the experience of visiting Max' Piano Bar. He largely avoids literal marine icons, seeking instead to suggest the experience of entering the hold of a submerged vessel through the use of particular materials and volumes.

Practical elements such as artists' changing rooms, staff toilets, kitchen and storage areas are all logically accommodated in the rectangular plan, which features a glass brick sinusoidal partition to screen the customer toilets. The furniture deserves special mention, consisting of chairs

originally designed in 1934 by Xavier Pouchard (and now reissued by the French firm of Fenêtre Sur Cour) and small bespoke tables designed by Piu himself. The bar counter is curved and defined by its dramatically stepped brass facing, while the stage – floating above the floor – also curves and features a kind of tubular ship's rail that proudly displays its welding. The cumulative effect is of a coherent design that began with its immersed metallic grotto imagery and then had to search for a location, instead of the other way around. Designer: **Pierluigi Piu**. Commissioning Client: **Giorgio Dessi**. Total Floor Space: **297 square metres**. Number of Levels: **1**. Contract Cost: **£170,000**. Completed: **Autumn 1997**.

opposite The metal sheeting of the bar interior evokes the submarine metaphor with a degree of subtlety. **below** The axonometric and section show boldness of approach to the basement location.

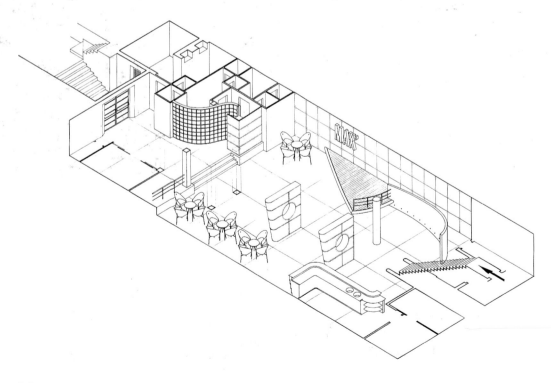

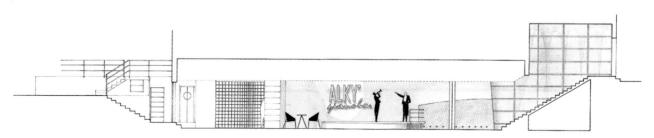

left and above A stepped brass bar counter and glass brick partition form key elements in the basement space.
opposite The displayed ship-style welding shown here in the descent to the bar suggests the idea of 'immersion'.

This project has its origins in the city of Berlin's unsuccessful bid to host the 2000 Olympic Games. The original plan was to build two sports halls at the Ludwig-Jahn Stadium in a rough district close to the Berlin Wall. When the Olympic bid stalled, only one project went ahead. The Max Schmeling Hall today is the venue not for Olympic athletes but for the Alba basketball team, which incongruously takes its name from the city's largest rubbish disposal company. But despite the downgrading of sporting expectation, the building by Joppien + Dietz deserves the highest billing. This young architectural practice from Frankfurt won an international competition to design the scheme against the odds, and then managed to build it successfully in the face of inevitable budget cuts as the Olympic dream faded.

The hall is actually built into the side of a mound of war rubble, so that it is almost completely buried in the landscape. Grass-covered roofs provide a link to the green areas of the adjacent sports grounds, while the central arena can be viewed from a square in front of the building through a giant transparent façade. Critics of the scheme argued that the underground nature of the facility would create a dark underworld, but the light-filled arena, much larger than it looks from the outside, is a bright and dynamic space able to accommodate up to 10,000 spectators.

The arena uses a restricted palette of three materials – steel, glass and concrete. Its stands are like tapered concrete scoops which appear to hang weightlessly in the air.

Above, an elegant steel-girder structural system spans a space that is 18 metres in height at the centre. Other sports facilities, including a dance centre and youth hall, are located off the central arena out of sight in the core of the building. The arena is clearly the main event. Despite the problematic nature of project and site, this is a leisure facility which is direct and full of clarity while showing a surprising amount of spatial guile.

Architect: **Joppien + Dietz**. Commissioning Client: **OSB** (Olympia Sportstätten Berlin). Total Floor Space: **24,852 square metres**. Contract Cost: **DM 205 million**. Completed: **1997**.

above The building façade is distinguished by its glass frontage and wedge-shaped roofline.
below The ground-floor plan shows the main arena flanked by adjacent sports facilities.
opposite The arena's entrance lobby.

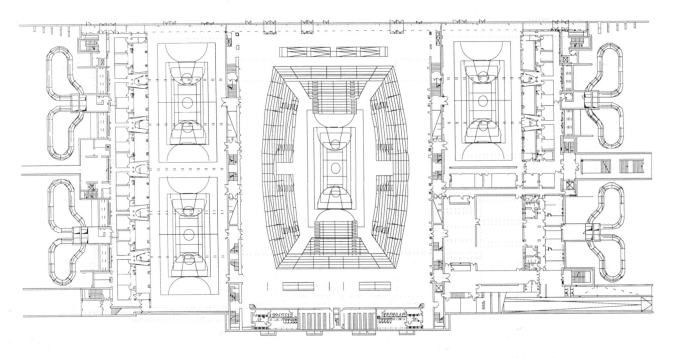

below Inside the main arena, which seats up to 10,000 spectators.

bottom The section reveals the steel-girder ceiling structure that spans the facility.

opposite The stands sit within the arena like tapered concrete scoops suspended weightlessly in space.

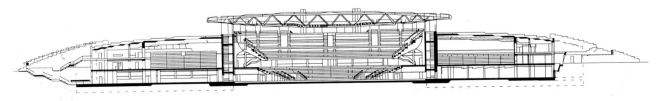

When London design practice BOA (Barber Osgerby Associates) was commissioned to create a modern interpretation of a traditional beer keller and restaurant for 250 people in a listed warehouse building, all structural alterations were off the menu. This was a tricky assignment, given that the scheme needed to include an open kitchen and all the functional aspects of a working brewery on site, as well as make the most of an unremarkable entrance and a brick-arched basement space with no natural light. But, despite such constraints, a brightly lit, modern industrial interior knits together the different elements of the scheme with a measured economy and a certain élan.

All internal fixtures and fittings, including a curved plywood wall, the brewery and furniture, were designed to be free-standing and independent of the building fabric. On the ground floor a special concrete slab was cast to support the heavy equipment needed to expose the brewing process to the public gaze, and a 17-metre-long, stainless-steel bar was produced in Germany for the project. Downstairs in the basement, bespoke plywood furniture – restaurant tables and chairs, banquette seating with concealed lighting, drinking shelves and stools – was designed by BOA and made by Windmill Furniture. The plywood stools are today manufactured by Herman Miller in the US.

This is a project in which huge water and fermentation tanks, piping and ductwork (all part of the micro-brewery) are constantly observed by large numbers of customers, many of whom have had a few drinks. So balancing aesthetic needs with those of safety and maintenance was never going to be simple. But BOA's solutions are as easy on the eye as they are hard-wearing.

Architect: **BOA (Barber Osgerby Associates)**.
Commissioning Client: **Soho Brewing Company**. Total Floor Space: **5,200 square feet**. Number of Levels: **2**. Contract Cost: **£750,000**. Completed: **May 1998**.

below The cross-section through the basement area and floor plan. The plan shows the arrangement of dining area and peripheral brewing facilities.
opposite The restaurant interior and section (below). Bespoke plywood furniture lends style and distinction to this impressive scheme.

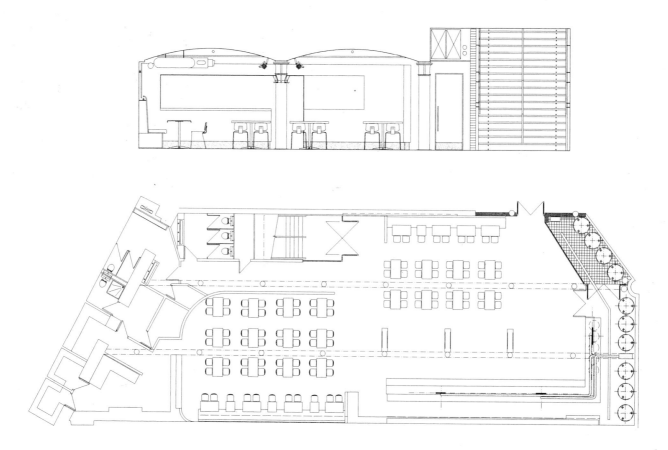

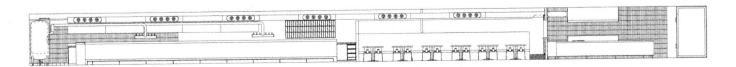

left The entrance to the eaterie.

opposite The micro-brewery which functions under the constant scrutiny of diners. The requirements involved in having a working brewery on site added a layer of technical complexity to the project.

3 retail

3.5

The narrative storyline of the *fin-de-siècle* arcade has arrived in perfect time for the new millennium.

A Dutch shopping centre reconstructs the medieval city while a Kent complex evokes the history of England in a series of courtly promenades.

Leather-covered staircases, mirrored furniture and perspex display cases suggest endless invention with the props of retailing.

Building the brand has become as much the work of the interior designer as of the marketer.

A backlash against designer minimalism in fashion retailing is promoting the use of colour and pattern.

Penetrating basement spaces with natural light is as important as creating artificial sources.

Some retail projects are determined to outdo Disney and Rockwell in their dynamism.

Other schemes are introducing a cooler, sharper, more industrial image based on transparency in dealing with the customer.

3.11

Bluewater is not a single retail interior. Instead it is a singularly spectacular architectural concept that not only reinvents the shopping mall by creating a series of unusual and inspirational promenades, but also signals 'the rebirth of storytelling in retail architecture', according to its designer, Eric Kuhne. The scale is vast. Bluewater is the stuff of legend, statistically as well as stylistically. It is the largest retail and leisure complex ever built in Europe, with more than 300 retail stores (as well as 14,000 square metres of leisure facilities) encased in a classicist's fantasyland that merges the Botanical Gardens with Burlington Arcade.

Kuhne's masterplan is triangular in shape to accommodate three anchor tenants (John Lewis Partnership, House of Fraser and Marks & Spencer) and it has three 'villages' at each of its three points. The eastern village is family- and child-oriented and includes the largest winter garden built in Britain in the twentieth century; the southern village has a media and entertainment theme aimed at teenagers and young adults; the western village has a more sophisticated image with health spa, gourmet food and high-end fashion accessory stores. On a chalk pit site landscaped with a million new trees and a 23-acre lake, double-level malls linking the three anchor stores are styled like balconied streets, infused with gentle light, ringed with ornamental balustrades and topped by handkerchief domes based on the interiors of Sir John Soane and Gilbert Scott. Three formal forecourts, inspired by the celestial themes of sun, moon and stars, create courtly anterooms to the anchor tenants. Shakespearean sonnets and quotations from Dickens, Keats and Chaucer are inscribed along the route. Bluewater's eccentric roofline, modelled on English stately homes, is silhouetted against chalk cliffs 50 metres high.

Kuhne, a son of modernism who has decisively rejected its universal ideology, has sought to recast the American shopping experience in the image of England's historic literature and landscape. To give the interiors such a narrative, he has marshalled an army of artesans, sculptors, craftsmen and ironsmiths from all over the UK and revitalized some crafts neglected for a generation or more. Store designers working for Bluewater's myriad tenants have been forced to project their own retail brands through this richly symbolic framework. Some have been maddened by what they see as clichéd views of Englishness. But Kuhne is unrepentant: 'At Bluewater, we're aiming to capture a British spirit embedded deep in the culture. Only the Church and the royals have ever done it properly – and I'm trying to do it with profane commercial buildings.'

Architect: **Eric R. Kuhne & Associates**. Commissioning Client: **Lend Lease**. Retail Floor Space: **154,000 square metres**. Total Contract Cost: **£700 million**. Completed: **March 1999**.

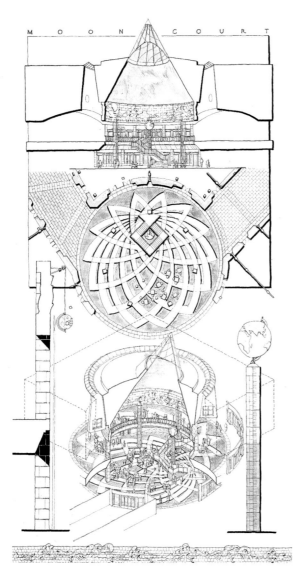

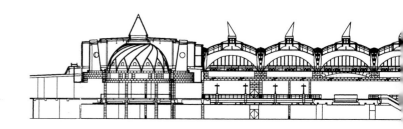

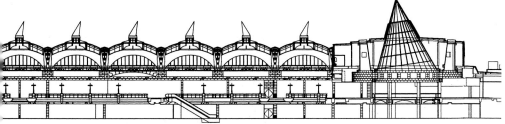

above English culture writ large at Bluewater.

opposite Concept diagram for the Moon Court and (left) a section through the east mall.

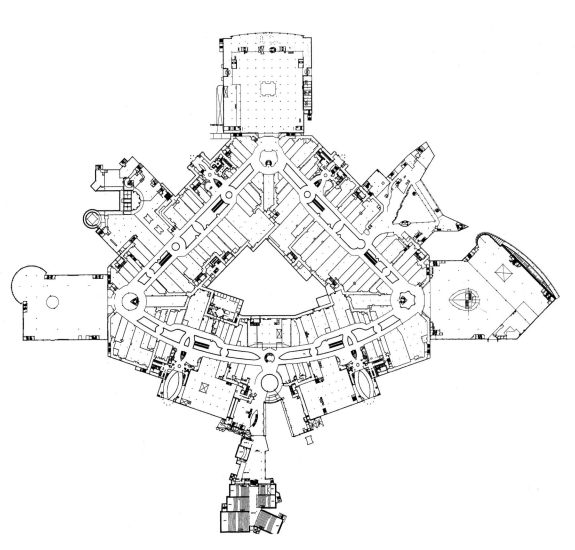

previous pages The Sun Court at the
junction of the east and west malls (left) with
its spectacular swirled ceiling (right).
above The triangular plan shows how three
anchor tenants are linked by decorative malls.

above A roof detail evokes the English stately home in abstract form. The architect's aim was to weave a narrative about the locality.

above left Sir John Soane and Gilbert Scott were the very English inspirations behind the balconied streets with their delicate domed and vaulted ceilings and ornamental balustrading.

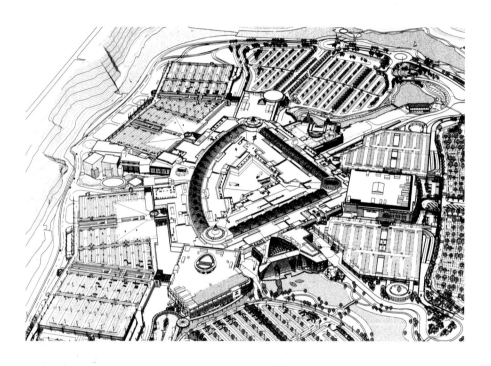

top left The site sketch reveals Bluewater's triangular plan and extensive carparking within a Kent chalk pit.

opposite and above Interior and exterior views of the largest winter gardens built in Britain in the 20th century. The composition is akin to a still life, according to the architect.

Antonio Citterio's architectural remodelling of the Aspesi fashion showroom on Via Brera in Milan creates an interior of such purity and lightness that it transcends commercial retailing and occupies that special ground between design studio and art gallery. The ground-level showroom unites a series of airy and austere rooms that were once service spaces in a patrician eighteenth-century Milanese residence of baroque origins. The building's fine features are retained as an immaculate white canvas to display not only Aspesi's clothes but works by such artists as Mario Merz, Andy Warhol, Mario Schifano, Mimmo Rotella and Jannis Kounnellis. The message is clear: fashion, which we hang on our bodies, is an art form on a par with art that we hang on a wall.

Citterio, working with Patricia Viel, uses economy of effect to frame this interior narrative. Existing walls are painted white, as are new plasterboard walls and ceilings. The pale flooring has been achieved with a confection of marble powders. The display system uses simple brushed stainless-steel tubes and white-painted wooden shelves with integral lighting. The whole setting benefits from a careful combination of direct and indirect lighting, including recessed Staff and I Guzzini spots, custom-designed Flos hanging lamps and fluorescent tubes recessed into niches. Furniture comprises aluminium chairs by Zanotta and tables by B&B Italia, with whom Citterio has enjoyed a long working relationship.

Indeed it is Citterio's pedigree as a designer of furniture and systems as well as spaces that makes the simplicity and rigour of this scheme so attractive. As a proponent of cool rationalism, who combines architecture and design so effectively, Citterio is widely regarded as the heir to the immediate post-war Italian legacy of Gio Ponti and Carlo Mollino. As he says, 'I am interested in a synthesis of ideas, in a process of reduction to the basic essentials. I still believe that less is more.' The Aspesi showroom proves this point.
Designers: **Antonio Citterio & Partners**. Commissioning Client: **Alberto Aspesi**. Total Floor Space: **300 square metres**. Number of Levels: **1**. Contract Cost: **Confidential**. Completed: **November 1997**.

opposite The fashion showroom as art gallery, utilizing the natural grace of an 18th-century Milanese residence. **below** Floor plan.

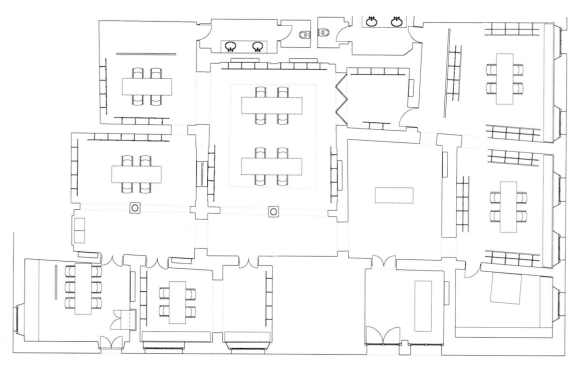

left and opposite A series of liquid
and austere rooms that convey a
strong message of artistic integrity.
below The main showroom area
with distinctive furniture by Zanotta
and B&B Italia enhancing the simple
elegance of the space.

The John G. Shedd Aquarium in Chicago seeks to promote the enjoyment, appreciation and conservation of aquatic life through research, education and public display. Every modern visitor attraction must have its gift store, and although the Aquarium likes to imply that its retail experience, Go Overboard, is part of an educational remit, the store's interior is one of uncomplicated fun which demands little in the way of study or learning. Schwartz Architects have risen to the challenge of the store's name by inserting a cable-suspended fibreglass giant octopus that weighs some 1,400 pounds and measures 28 feet across and 14 feet high. The octopus grips eight structural columns in a playful embrace, setting the tone for a mock underwater environment.

Go Overboard boasts five themed departments rather idiosyncratically labelled as Coral Reef, Rain Forest, Shedd Architecture, Kids and Books, with fixtures radiating from the hovering octopus. More oversized sea creatures are three dimensionally realized in fibreglass and perch on top of marine-flavoured fixtures with sandblasted glass shelves. Visitors unfazed by the sight of a four-foot-high shrimp or an Emperor Penguin the size of a sumo wrestler can navigate their way through the store's different sales areas by referring to the frieze of laser-cut signage. In the book department, which targets adults, each free-standing book fixture supports large tinted and etched Lucite panels with images and text from famous works of maritime literature (e.g., *Moby Dick* and *Treasure Island*).

Spot- and floodlights are used throughout for general lighting, which unifies the whole environment. Underwater effects are achieved with metal halide projectors using custom split-dichroic filters and water-ripple effect attachments. The free-standing merchandise units with the giant sea creatures are illuminated by 12-volt tight spots, while photomurals are lit with high-temperature, compact fluorescent track lights. The client brief was simply 'to out-Rock Rockwell and out-Dis Disney' and increase sales fourfold.

Designers: **Schwartz Architects, with Esherick Homsey Dodge & Davis** Commissioning Client: **The John G. Shedd Aquarium**. Total Floor Space: **5,700 square feet**. Number of Levels: **1**. Contract Cost: **$1.6 million** (including base building infrastructure). Completed: **May 1998**.

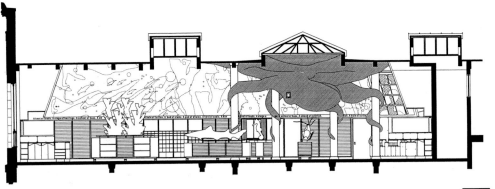

left and below Section and floor plan show a scheme in the grip of a giant octopus. **opposite** Other oversized sea creatures make the hard sell in Go Overboard.

key

1	kids area	a	shrimp
2	computers	b	seahorse
3	architecture	c	iguana
4	books	d	sea turtle
5	rain forest	e	leopard shark
6	coral reef	f	tree frog
		g	moray eel
		h	porcupine fish
		i	clown triggerfish
		j	penguin
		k	giant octopus

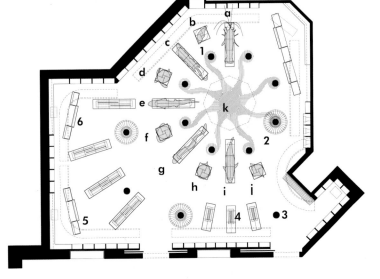

flamingos. A sw... . An army of frog

Seahorse

this page The giant octopus in concept and
final form. Despite the store's educational
remit, the emphasis is on uncomplicated fun.
overleaf The cash and wrap station in
seaweed green plywood with video display
and photo mural above (left). The book
department where etched Lucite panels
contain images and extracts from works by
Melville, Stevenson and Verne (right).

Treasure Island

I now felt for the first time the joy of exploration. The isle was uninhabited; my shipmates I had left behind, and nothing lived in front of me but dumb brutes and fowls. I turned hither and thither among the trees. Here and there were flowering plants, unknown to me: here and there I saw snakes, and one raised his head from a ledge of rock and hissed at me with a noise not unlike the spinning of a top. Little did I suppose that he was a deadly enemy, and that the noise was the famous rattle.

STEVENSON

20,000 Leagues Under the Sea

Various kinds of isis, clustered of pure tuft-coral, prickly fungi, and anemones, formed a brilliant garden of flowers, enamelled with porphitae, decked with their collarettes of blue tentacles, sea-stars studding the sandy bottom, together with asterophytons like fine lace embroidered by the hands of naiads, whose festoon were waved by the gentle undulations caused by our walk.

VERNE

The transformation of Bradford's historic Wool Exchange into a mixed-use development with a Waterstone's bookshop in its Gothic main hall is a fitting symbol for the passage from the industrial to the information age of one of Britain's grittiest northern cities. Architects Dempster Thrussell and Rae have intervened in the Grade I-listed building with the lightest of touches, inserting modern additions that make no attempt to mimic the existing structure and can be easily removed in the future without adversely affecting the Victorian splendour of the site.

The original Wool Exchange is the imposing work of Bradford architects Lockwood and Mawson. John Ruskin advised on its triangular plan and Lord Palmerston, the Prime Minister, laid its foundation stone in 1864. The building was completed in 1867, but within 30 years, its ornate, carved façade, north-facing onto Hustlergate, had been substantially amended. A three-storey section was removed and replaced by a poorly detailed infill of little architectural merit which did not align with the original and let in rainwater.

A century later, this inadequate infill, which had led to extensive deterioration, was targeted by Dempster Thrussell and Rae as part of the restoration. After lengthy consultation with historic buildings watchdog English Heritage and the local planning authority, a frameless glass 'shop window' to showcase the bookshop and hall was designed. A new entrance was created from Hustlergate into the Gothic hall, where the simple wooden bookshelves of Waterstone's are reminiscent of a college library. With the primary shopping route in place, a new lightweight staircase was also inserted, leading to the upper floors where perimeter offices are grouped around the void over the main hall and a design studio space faces onto Hustlergate. This is a scheme that not only developed a modern retail environment in an evocative Victorian setting, but also delivered a design studio so attractive that the architects chose to take it for themselves as their Bradford base.

Designer: **Dempster Thrussell and Rae**. Commissioning Client: **Maple Grove Developments**. Total Floor Space: **Unavailable** Number of levels: **3**. Contract Cost: **£2.5 million**. Completed: **1997**.

below View of the new glazed façade from Hustlergate and a section through the scheme.

opposite A branch of Waterstone's booksellers occupies the Gothic splendour of the main hall.

key
1 office/studio
2 mezzanine (Waterstone's)
3 recessed external space
4 main hall (Waterstone's)
5 basement retail/food & drink
6 offices

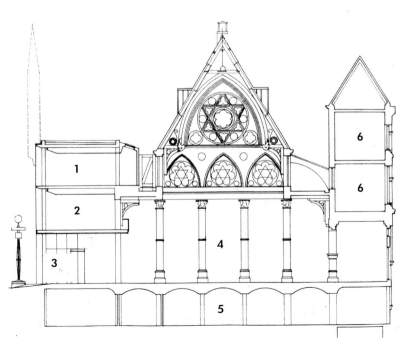

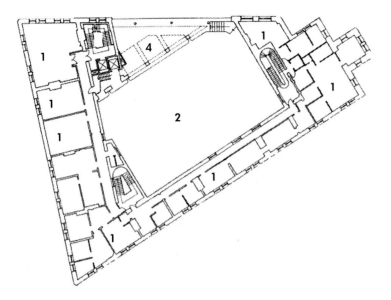

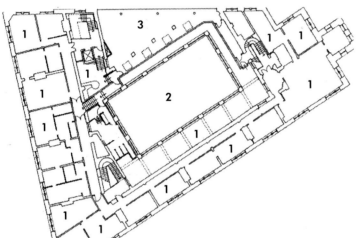

left First and second floor plans

opposite New lightweight stairs create a modern insertion into the historic building which owes its form to the ideas of John Ruskin.

below A studio space with views of Hustlergate became the architects' own base in Bradford.

key
1 offices
2 void over main hall
  (Waterstone's bookshop)
3 design studio
4 balcony to Waterstone's

3.5 rlb citybank innsbruck, austria

Retail banks belong distinctively to the modern age, but the new RLB Citybank at Innsbruck has an architectural provenance dating back to 1765. That was when the city gate was torn down and replaced with an architectural marker; a century later that was integrated into a structure that became an art dealer's house. The building now houses a bank with a very contemporary retail approach. The task facing architect Peter Lorenz was to create an interior that signalled the bank's commercial aims whilst making minimal impact upon an historic building.

Out of necessity, very little could be changed on the outside; only an extension at the rear was added and this complements the historical appearance of the building. Inside, the broad spatial arrangements involve three levels: strongroom and ancillary rooms in the basement; a 24-hour banking facility with ATMs and a general public concourse on the ground floor; and client consulting rooms on the first floor. The three areas are linked by a full-height plenum that is partly given over to a glazed lift.

Lorenz's aim was to project the bank's image in a way that would remove the need for what he calls 'the usual flamboyance of uninspired advertising artwork'. Going for a modern, friendly, urbane look, he decided to pre-empt the kind of decoration that traditionally gets applied after the architect has left, by introducing two young artists early in the planning process. Brigitte Kowanz contributed subtle decorative motifs that evoke the bank's logo, as well as two 'light-clocks' that play optical games with the idea of analogue and digital numerals, reinforcing the 24-hour theme. To separate the daytime and 24-hour zones on the cramped ground floor, Lorenz commissioned artist Eva Schlegel to create etched glass panels that can be parked to one side by day and rolled into position at night. The panel etchings depict the text of an actual loan-contract that has been tactfully stylized into illegibility.

Architect: **Peter Lorenz**. Artists: **Brigitte Kowanz, Eva Schlegel**. Commissioning Client: **Raiffeisen Landesbank Tirol**. Total Floor Space: **200 square metres**. Number of Levels: **3**. Contract Cost: **£500,000**. Completed: **December 1996**.

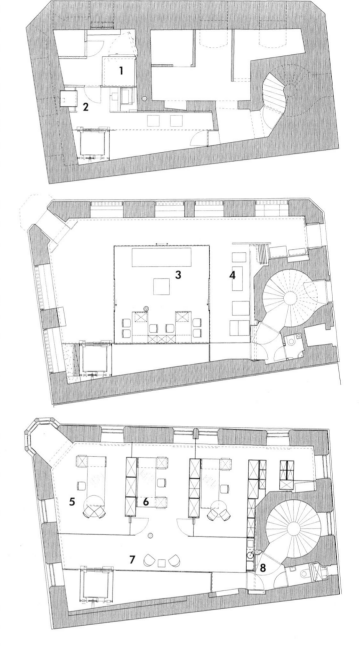

above top to bottom The basement, ground and first floor plans.

opposite Etched glass panels form an artistic element in the bank interior. A loan contract stylized into illegibility creates the pattern.

key
1 vault
2 safety deposit boxes
3 glass box
4 automated banking area
5 office
6 reception
7 waiting area
8 kitchen

above Artists were introduced early in the design process with the result that these 'light clocks' announce the bank's high-street presence.

opposite The bank interior projects a contemporary retail image within a building that dates back to 1765.

Nike Town has been one of the hottest retail design stories of the past decade. The Chicago and New York stores, opened in 1992 and 1996, respectively, set a new benchmark for brand manufacturers moving into retailing and sparked the high-street battle of the running shoe. The Nike Town concept is strong on information, education and customer feedback, with each store assuming museum or gallery-like characteristics to express Nike's heritage and communicate the sheer adrenalin of sport through ambient sound and image. This philosophy has been introduced to London in a joint project between the multidisciplinary practice BDP and Nike's design teams in Beaverton, USA, and Hilversum, Holland.

In a prime-site Grade II-listed building at Oxford Circus, Nike's retail offer has been given a London architectural and sporting 'spin' to add local flavour to a global brand. Local London 'homes of sport' were researched as part of a project which has at its core an electronic Nike pavilion symbolizing the future of Nike technology and containing the main structural, servicing, lighting and audio-visual elements required to give the store its constantly changing environment of image, sound and display. This vertical element, built using a palette of standard materials and inserted through substantial openings cut in the main floor plates, is reached from two of the three main trading floors

across metal bridges. It gives the scheme its unifying purpose; other pavilion 'buildings', each dedicated to a different sport, are grouped around the 'town square' it creates.

These pavilions use a wide variety of materials and finishes. Flooring includes granite, epoxy resin, terrazzo, timber, rubber and carpet. Internal dry-stud partition walls are faced with 'exterior' materials such as brick, metal and glass block to enhance the town square idea. Ceilings are treated individually from pavilion to pavilion: woven aluminium tubes depict a tennis racquet; pre-formed plywood reveals the contour lines of a map; there are also perforated metal and fabric tent ceilings. After New York, London was always fixed in Nike's sights as a flagship. Accordingly, Oxford Circus has been built with great energy, flair and attention to detail. The next Nike Town will be in Tokyo.

Designer: **BDP and Nike Retail Design**. Commissioning Client: **Nike Retail**. Total Floor Space: **70,000 square feet** Number of Levels: **3.** Contract Cost: **Confidential**. Completed: **June 1999**.

opposite The interior view shows the metal deck bridge connecting the Nike pavilion at the core of the project.
below Ground-floor and second-floor plans.

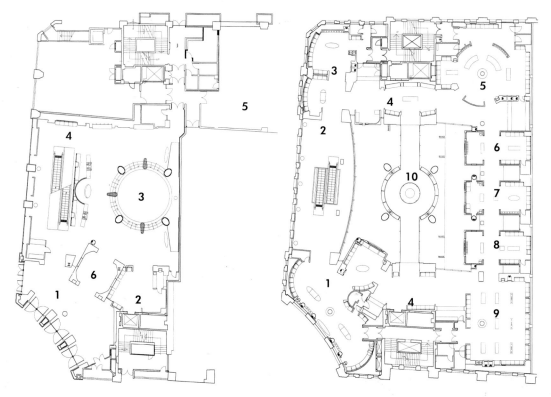

ground floor
1 entry
2 Niketown shop
3 Nike pavilion
4 archive pavilion
5 service area
6 induction area

second floor
1 all-conditions gear
2 archive pavilion
3 women's fitness
4 accessories
5 women's tennis
  and running
6 women's team sports
7 kids
8 boys
9 men's fitness
10 Nike pavilion

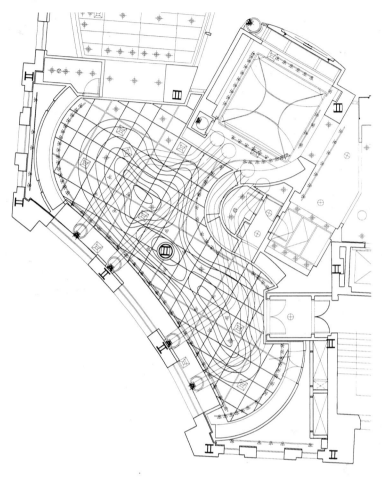

previous pages The brick-faced sports pavilion looks
on to the Nike pavilion, a dynamic technological
spine that extends vertically through the store.
opposite Nike merchandise is projected strongly in
an educational, gallery-style setting.
above Ground-floor view through the induction
area to Nike pavilion.
right Ceiling plan for all-conditions merchandise.
below Floor finishes for the archive pavilion.

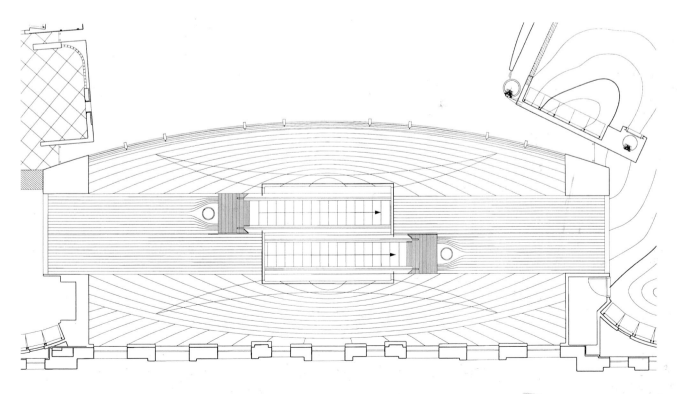

3.7 `virmani fashion shop` munich, germany

This is a small project for a fashion client of Indian origin. But according to designers Stephan Lang and Uwe Binnberg of Design Associates, it takes a big stand against what they perceive to be the uniformity of 'the minimal concept of modern shop design'. This minimalism is especially evident in fashion retailing where a kneejerk sparseness can often mask an absence of design inspiration.

There is no such shortage of creative ideas in the Virmani scheme, however. Taking the ethnicity of the client as its starting point, the store eschews cool, neutral modernity in favour of a vibrant artistic play on materials, patterns, treatments and craftsmanship. The single-floor outlet for the Virmani collection encompasses the main boutique with reception desk, changing rooms, storage and an office. The coloured, concrete-slab flooring inlaid with a pebble mosaic belongs to an overall palette that includes white plaster walls, bleached teak boards, white glass, antique Indian doors and columns and an antique limestone stair.

Within this authentic setting, s-shaped, brass-tipped steel rods with brass wall-connectors provide a practical and engaging display system for the clothing. Lighting consists of a combination of functional Kreon spots and two decorative golden pendant lights by Catallani and Smith. Indeed it is the marriage of the utilitarian with the ethnic and ornamental that gives this scheme its distinction. The designers wanted the store to say as much about the individuality of its customers as the individuality of the fashion. In this they have succeeded. As they observe, 'fashion sells by emotion', whereas too many minimalist shops bleed all feeling from the interior.
Designers: **Design Associates**. Commissioning Client: **Virmani Pradeep**. Total Floor Space: **120 square metres** Number of Levels: **1**. Contract Cost: **£75,000**. Completed: **May 1998**.

opposite and overleaf
The Virmani shop takes a stand against modern minimalism with its ethnic virtuosity, s-shaped display rods and pebble-mosaic flooring.
below The floor plan.

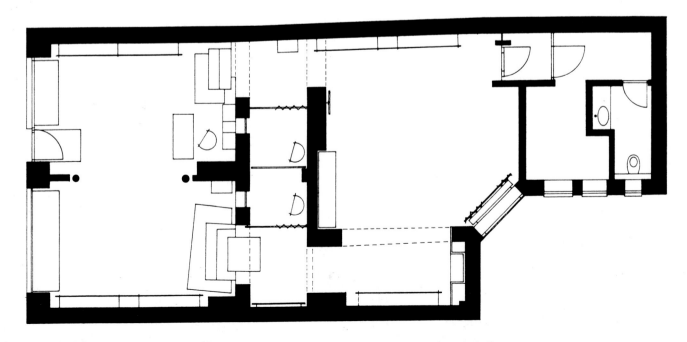

The creation of a strong national brand identity was the catalyst when Space NK Apothecary, which owns nine successful London stores, commissioned designers Virgile & Stone to develop its proven contemporary cosmetics format for a programmed UK expansion. An important aspect of the brief was to create definition between the product ranges and services to enable the concept to be applied to larger sites.

The concept was prototyped for the Trafford Centre in Manchester, UK and has continued to be developed through sites in Leeds, Birmingham, Glasgow and a new store in West London. The resulting solution establishes a light, bright, inviting atmosphere with a clear palette of finishes. Attention to detail ensures a quality feel, but broadly the impact is of airy modernity, the retail equivalent of a Manhattan loft. One particular objective was to make product groups clearly distinguishable without the use of signage. The products are identifiable by their position within the store, which is divided into three main areas using distinctive architectural elements to indicate product groups: a feature wall holds body and bath products; a cube wall contains skincare and men's products, and a coloured area signifies make-up.

There are no sharp divisions between retailer and customer, and floor units are accessible from both sides. The store's main light fittings are mounted in slots to create a clean and ordered ceiling line. A make-up testing area uses colour-changing fluorescent units to simulate day and night. For the wall displays, lighting is integrated into the back of the shelving in order to highlight products, while halo lighting of merchandise walls is used to stress the height and spaciousness of the premises.

Designer: **Virgile & Stone Associates**. Commissioning Client: **Space NK Apothecary**. Total Floor Space: **115 square metres.** Number of Levels: **1.** Contract Cost: **£143,000**. Completed: **October 1998**.

above Modernist clarity creates an uncluttered retail environment.

right Floor plan and sections show a highly ordered arrangement of products.

key
1 feature wall – body/bath/home/fragrance
2 cube wall – skincare/men's
3 colour wall – make-up
4 window display
5 tester units/promotional display
6 cash unit

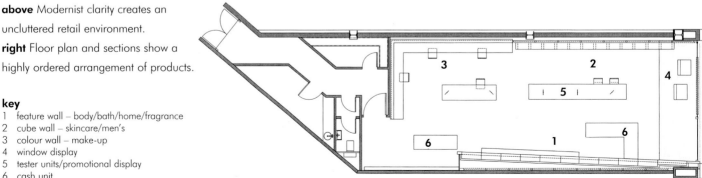

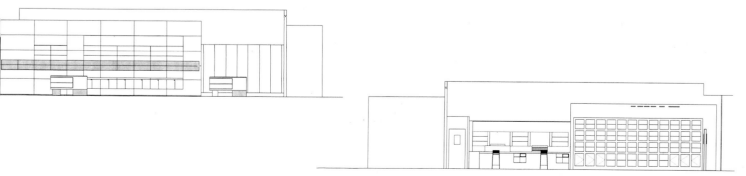

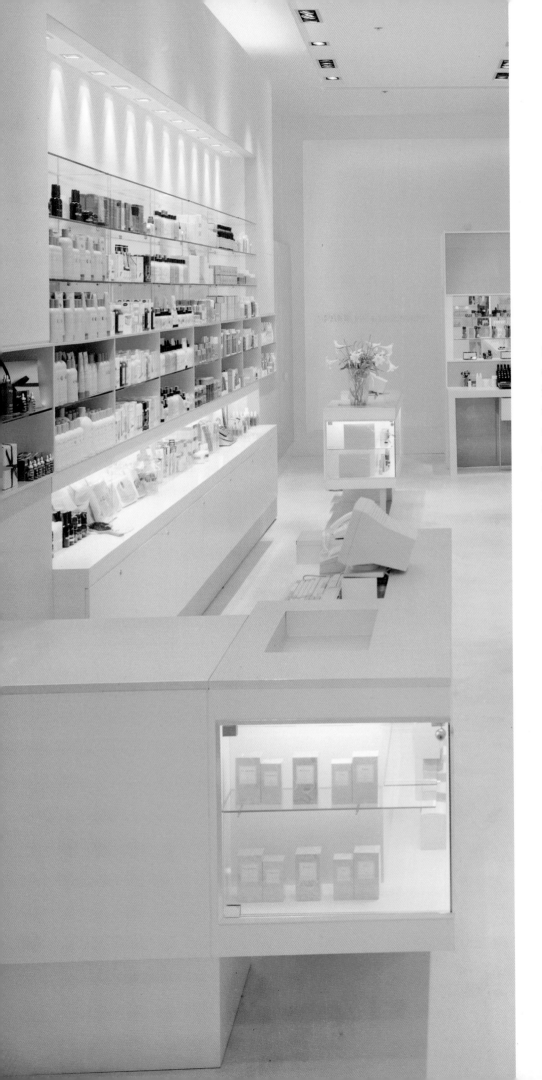

left A cube wall holds skincare and men's products in neutral frames that rationally promote the merchandise.
opposite The design strategy seeks to communicate the quality values of the Space NK brand in a trading format that can be rolled out across the UK.

The de Barones shopping centre is the central element in an ambitious attempt to reconstruct the heart of a medieval city in southern Holland. Known as the de Barones project, this complex scheme took five years to complete and involved cooperation between the local Welstandcommissie (a body concerned with the aesthetic quality of new projects), two architectural practices, a client group consisting of a developer and local council, and the owners of an existing store on the site.

CZWG's responsibility was for the design of the arterial shopping mall that provides the focus for this subtle exercise in restoration, demolition, student housing and retail development, all coming together within an historic setting. An old library building (listed as an example of the Amsterdam School) was incorporated into the retail scheme where its structural frame remained intact, leaving CZWG to create a new volume celebrating this distinguished reinforced concrete frame structure. The retail store Habitat became the revamped library's anchor tenant from the first floor upwards. Otherwise CZWG has made the two-storey shopping centre a practical and uncluttered retail space, free from ersatz decoration (despite a rather whimsical giant open-weave terracotta 'curtain' suspended on the façade above the Niewstraat entrance).

Materials used inside are all prefabricated with dry natural finishes such as precast concrete, oak, steel, terracotta and granite. The overall organization is not that of the conventional extended mall, but rather a linked collection of individual spaces, each with its own roof of glazed steel trusses. What looks like a monumental central column is something of a tease since it is only partially structural: in fact it stops short above ground floor level acting as a duct for ventilation and providing seating around its base. Like all good *fin-de-siècle* arcades, de Barones sports an interior that takes the first-time visitor by surprise: nothing of this scale and quality is suggested by the exterior.

Architect: **CZWG** (with Kraaijvanger Urbis).
Commissioning Client: **MAB BV, Vroom and Dreesmann Nederland, Municipality of Breda, owner CGI**. Total Floor Space: **42,000 square metres**. Number of Levels: **2**. Contract Cost: **£25 million**. Completed: **September 1997**.

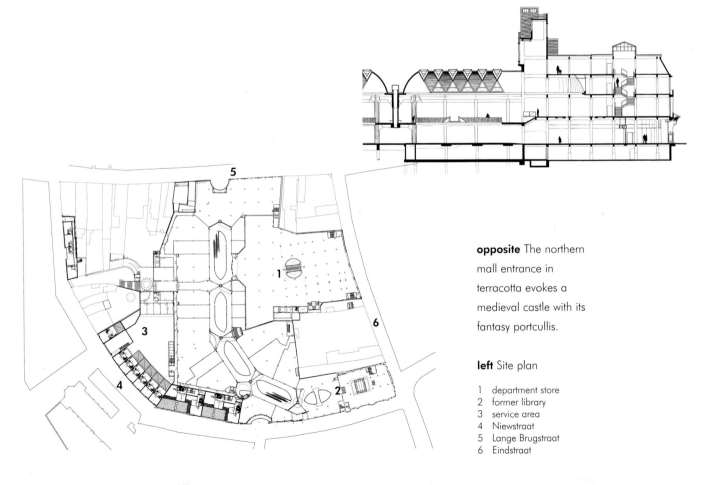

opposite The northern mall entrance in terracotta evokes a medieval castle with its fantasy portcullis.

left Site plan

1 department store
2 former library
3 service area
4 Niewstraat
5 Lange Brugstraat
6 Eindstraat

left The mall interior combines style with practicality. Columns at first-floor level contain ventilation ducts and have integral seating and lighting.

opposite A view across the oak upper floor towards anchor tenant Habitat which occupies the old library space.

3.10 bene showroom london, uk

In 1997 Apicella Associates designed a small London show-room for Bene Office Furniture. Recently Lorenzo Apicella, his practice now part of Pentagram, returned to the showroom to expand and update it. To do this he added to the street-level space a tanked-out, lower-ground level 'design laboratory'. The additional area is intended for Bene to display its Working Walls partitioning systems, and for its clients to try out combinations of furniture from the Bene range.

In creating the additional level, Apicella also reposi-tioned the entrance to the original showroom so that it now also offers access to the new lower level. Now the visitor can climb the small perforated steel staircase up to the reception desk on the (slightly raised) street-level floor, or descend to the new lower level with its raised galvanized steel floor and bare white walls. Considerable daylight penetrates the glass entrance and perforated steel stairs, making the lower level lighter than might be expected. Natural light is also maxi-mized by placing mirrors in the soffits of a clerestory at street level, helping to illuminate recesses that extend beneath the pavement which are used for the display of individual office setups. Glass partitions separate this zone from the rest of the lower-level space.

Overall, the style and palette of the newly expanded premises reflects Bene's evolving image. Although a few planes of blue, red and yellow remain from the previous design, the new premises are generally cooler, brighter and more industrially chic. The designation of the new lower level as a 'playground' for customers also says something about the client's creative aspirations.

Designer: **Pentagram**. Commissioning Client: **Bene Office Furniture**. Total Floor Space: **350 square metres**. Number of Levels: **2**. Contract Cost: **Confidential**. Completed: **September 1998**.

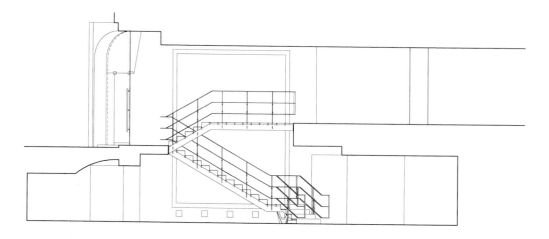

above A view through the lower-ground-floor 'design laboratory' with raised steel floor.

opposite Section.

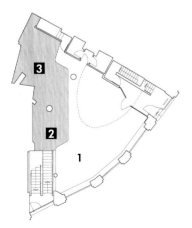

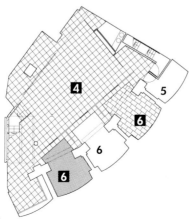

Ground-floor plan
1 showroom
2 reception
3 meeting room

Lower-ground-floor plan
4 showroom and presentation area
5 store
6 display

left and right The new, expanded premises reveal a cooler and brighter showroom projecting a chic industrial image.
below Daylight penetrates the lower level.
below right The Bene entrance defines two routes, up or down, for visitors.

Alexandre Hercovitch is considered the most talented Brazilian fashion designer on the contemporary scene. Nevertheless, despite such tremendous acclaim, there was only a modest budget for the new Hercovitch shop in São Paulo and a similarly minimal floor area for interior designer Arthur de Mattos Casas to work with. It is to the scheme's credit that it manages to do so much with so little – the interior architectural equivalent of the little black dress or the singular white t-shirt.

Within a tight, triangular floor plan of just 50 square metres, Arthur de Mattos Casas makes extensive use of mirrors to amplify the space, incorporating them into everything from table tops to acrylic chairs of his own design. The acrylic flooring is colour-matched to the walls, creating a sense of continuous, infinite space. Within this enhanced volume, the architect has developed a flexible set that can be rearranged at will to suit to the latest Hercovitch collection.

Distinctive features include a series of vertical chromed metal rods suspended from the ceiling, from which the clothing is hung, and smart, moveable medium-density fibreboard door panels. Working with collaborating designer Silvia Carmesini, de Mattos Casas has also produced a soft, ambient lighting scheme – all part of a project dedicated to making sure that it is Hercovitch's clothing, and not the retail design, that is the star attraction.

Designers: **Studio Arthur de Mattos Casas**.
Commissioning Client: **Alexandre Hercovitch**. Total Floor Space: **50 square metres**. Number of Levels: **2**. Contract Cost: **US$50,000**. Completed: **November 1998**.

opposite The fashion store uses economy of means to turn on the style.
below The floor plan reveals the tight triangular form of the Hercovitch retail outlet.

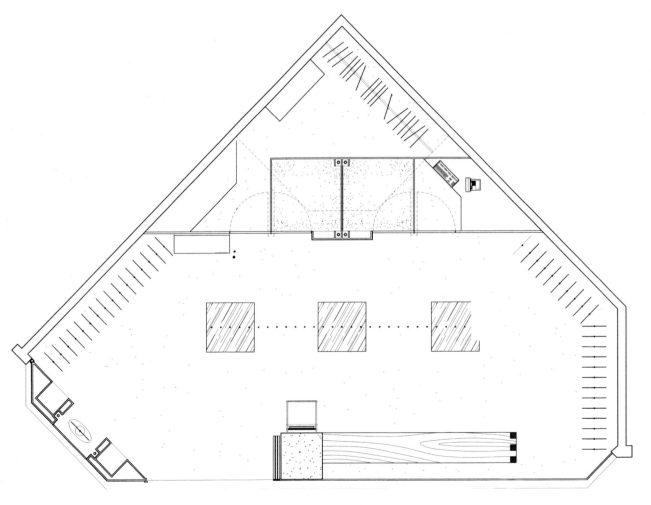

above and opposite A flexible stage set that can be
reconfigured at will with each new Alexandre Hercovitch
Collection features moveable hangers and panels.

The Lille boutique of Hermès, one of the smartest names in French luxury goods, has occupied a small early seventeenth-century Flemish baroque building on the Rue de la Grande Chaussée since 1977. When Hermès acquired space adjoining this site, the opportunity to extend the sales area needed to be balanced against the historical constraints of a structure managed by the conservation body Bâtiments de France. Designer Rena Dumas was as concerned with retaining the charm of the original Hermès boutique as the authorities were with preserving the building. The result is a scheme of sensitivity and skill, in which the warmth of the Flemish house is expressed in a new language of modernity.

Architecturally, Dumas and her design team unified the façade on the ground floor in its original style, restoring missing parts of the pillars and stone arches. The façade of the upper floors was totally rebuilt in sculpted limestone and brick in Flemish baroque style. The stone was painted in yelow ochre and the brick in pink, according to the specifications of Bâtiments de France. The wall between the original boutique and the extension was pierced with three large flat-arched openings, and a brick wall enclosure encircling the stairs of the original shop was preserved in its original state but linked to a newly created two-level portico behind the façade. The effect is to open up a view into an internal courtyard where a steel-and-glass skylight draws light deep into the boutique, creating a sense of communication between the ground and first floors.

The artistic heritage of Hermès is one of leather craftsmanship. This is reflected in a spectacular leather-covered staircase that links the two main sales levels. The ground floor immediately greets the visitor with a classic collection of leather goods, as well as silk scarves and ties. The first floor displays men and women's ready-to-wear, jewellery, watch-making and the art of the table. With their wooden parquet flooring and walls of copper-toned French Cherry panelling, the sales areas are simple and distinctive. Rena Dumas is part of the Hermès clan – the Greek designer married into the family in 1962. But she has shown a great deal of objectivity here in distilling and communicating the essence of Hermès' enduring appeal.

Designers: **Rena Dumas Architecture Intérieure**. Commissioning Client: **Hermès**. Total Floor Space: **6,500 square feet**. Number of Levels: **2**. Contract Cost: **Confidential**. Completed: **October 1997**.

left The architect's rendering reveals the sensitive restoration of the 17th-century Flemish baroque building.
opposite The spectacular leather-clad staircase which links the two main sales areas. It also connects with Hermès' saddlery heritage.

above The steel-and-glass skylight which crowns an internal courtyard, revealing a view of the upper sales floor.
opposite The delicate form of the leather staircase.

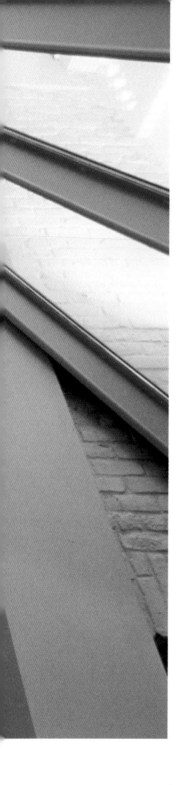

3.13 **issey miyake pleats please** london, uk

This store on London's Brook Street is the smallest of several which the Stanton Williams practice has designed for Japanese fashion guru Issey Miyake. And with its long, narrow layout, low ceiling and poky basement area, it can't have been the easiest to work with. But the Pleats Please shop, dedicated to the Pleats Please range of clothes and accessories (which are distinguished by strong colours and geometric shapes), overcomes the constraints of the domestically proportioned spaces of a Georgian townhouse in a way that is engaging, practical and innovative.

Customers are enticed deep into the store by a large video screen, set in a backlit etched-glass wall, that provides a constantly changing show of Miyake's latest creations. During the day this makes for a shimmering sense of animation, which complements the stronger abstract lines of white light in the ceiling; at night it promotes Pleats Please onto the street. To encourage people to venture into the basement, Stanton Williams cut a large glazed strip into the ground floor which allows natural light to filter down through the horizontal sliding perspex planes of the inventive display units that hold the pleated garments as rolls of fabric. This opening, integrated with the staircase, effectively creates a double-height space for those in the basement and provides views back up through the translucent and colour-filled displays.

A sense of transparency was key to the project. The designers describe the store as a 'light box'; its plain white walls and perspex and stainless-steel units highlight the boldness and brightness of the clothes. The pleated fabrics themselves are put to functional use as, for example, curtains on changing rooms. This is Stanton Williams' fourth Issey Miyake store, part of a body of work which is a diversion from its usual preoccupation with museum and exhibition spaces. But it definitely belongs in a portfolio which is all about suitability and design excellence.
Designers: **Stanton Williams**. Commissioning Client: **Issey Miyake London.** Total Floor Space: **94 square metres.** Number of Levels: **2**. Contract Cost: **Confidential.** Completed: **May 1997.**

above A video screen set in a backlit etched glass wall at the rear of the store draws visitors in from the entrance.
opposite The view into the basement sales area shows the visual access to the upper level achieved by cutting a large glazed strip in the ground floor.
below Section (below, top) and plans of the ground floor (below, centre) and basement (bottom).

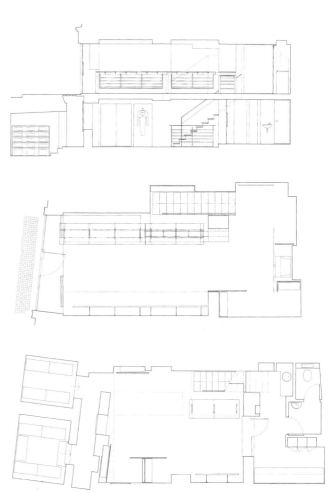

opposite Custom-designed perspex display units
allow natural light to filter down through
transparent horizontal planes.

above The view from the basement level gives
the impression of a double-height space due to
the effect of the sculptural glazed opening.

4 public

4.2

4.8

Public interiors are dissolving the boundaries between inside and out, and between old and new.

A German cinema embraces the neighbourhood, a New Mexico theatre embraces the landscape.

Historic structures are being given ambitious makeovers; an old market becomes a literary centre; an old playhouse, a multiplex.

Beaux Arts libraries and listed museums are being twinned with challenging contemporary extensions.

Airport terminals are discovering a local sense of identity after decades of soulless multinational design.

The focus of public spaces is democratic and inclusive rather than monolithic and impressive.

Galleries are playing with light and perspective, as organic forms soften the image of public buildings.

The slashed face of Berlin's Jewish Museum is as much a symbol of Germany's past as the Reichstag dome is of the country's future.

4.10

Agonized over by Holocaust experts and survivors for almost a quarter of a century, the Jewish Museum in Berlin bears the terrible weight of genocidal history perhaps more heavily than any other building in the last years of the twentieth century. Even the choice of Daniel Libeskind as architect, following a competition held in 1988–9, was a poignant one: Libeskind, who was born in 1946 just a few hundred kilometres east of Berlin in Lodz, Poland, lost most of his family in the Holocaust. That the resulting museum is not simply an essay on dislocation and loss but is also able to inspire a sense of moral optimism for the future is testament to Libeskind's special powers as a designer of hauntingly bleak and poetic spaces.

The site of the Jewish Museum is on the Lindenstrasse close to what was the Berlin Wall and next door to the distinguished Collegienhaus, the old baroque Prussian courthouse. Its zinc-clad façade, slashed as if by some vicious attack, contrasts with its near neighbour, the gashes in its walls sending splintered patterns of random light deep into recesses of the interior galleries. The entrance through the Collegienhaus leads into a dramatic entry void by a stair which descends under the existing building foundations, crisscrosses underground and materializes above ground as an independent building.

Libeskind has called his scheme 'Between The Lines' because, as he explains, 'it is a project about two lines of thinking, organization and relationship. One is a straight line but broken into many fragments; the other is a tortuous line but continues indefinitely'. He was determined to reflect Berlin's historic cultural, economic and intellectual debt to its Jewish citizens in his building design, and has drawn on four profound ideas in its development. First is the plotting of an 'irrational matrix' of connections between Jewish life and German history in the city, so revealing in the plan a compressed and contorted yellow star, symbolizing those which the Jews were forced to wear in Nazi Berlin. Second is a reference to Berlin composer Schoenberg's unfinished opera *Moses and Aaron*, which Libeskind sought to complete archi-

tecturally. Third is a dimension that reflects his interest in Berliners who were deported and murdered under the Nazis, a subject which he researched extensively. The fourth aspect is called 'One Way Street' and features Walter Benjamin's text on urban apocalypse revealed in a continuous sequence along the museum's zig-zag form.

The museum has three underground 'roads', which tell their own stories but give no hint of their destinations. One leads to the main exhibition spaces and the continuation of Berlin's history. Another leads outdoors to the ETA Hoffman Garden, symbolic of exile and emigration. The third leads to a dead end – the chilling Holocaust void. In an echo of deportation horrors, visitors push through solid metal doors to reach an unknown destination. Each gallery space is negotiated by a bridge across a void, the fragility and emptiness of the environment reflecting the precarious and dehumanized world into which Berlin's Jews were plunged.

Designer: **Studio Daniel Libeskind**. Commissioning Client: **Berlin Senate of Culture**. Total Floor Space: **155,000 square feet**. Number of Levels: **4**. Contract Cost: **US$40.05 million**. Completed: **January 1999**.

above The Jewish Museum's slashed zinc-clad façade contrasts with the stately Collegienhaus.
below A section through the great stair which links the galleries.
opposite A view of the arterial 'void' passages that link the public areas.

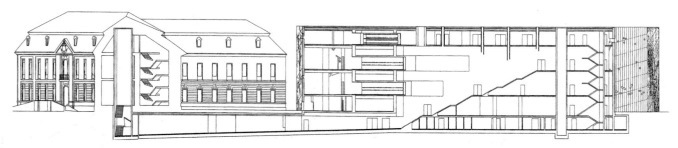

above The passageway suggests the precariousness of fate.
opposite The gallery space with the evocative slashes of the façade showing through is infused with poetic lines of light.

left and opposite The Jewish Museum's extraordinary exterior speaks eloquently of the savagery that led to the suffering of Berlin's Jews.
below The building is sited next to the ETA Hoffman Garden, a sculptural symbol of exile.
bottom The first-floor plan reveals a design that suggests a contorted Star of David.

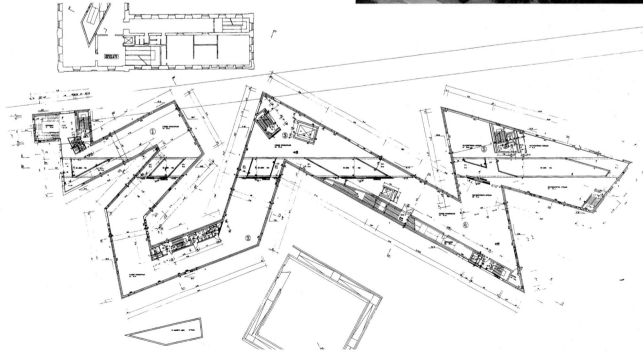

Cleveland's neoclassical Main Library was built in 1925 to adhere to the principles of a visionary 1903 scheme intended to ensure visual harmony for the city's Beaux Arts civic buildings. By the 1990s, renovation and expansion were necessary in order to enhance library services. Architects Hardy Holzman Pfeiffer Associates (HHPA) were appointed to renovate the Main Library and almost double overall capacity with the addition of a new building, the Louis Stokes Wing.

The Main Library renovation includes the restoration of historic elements such as decorative paint-stencilled ceilings, murals, marble wainscoting, and original fittings and furnishings. Some new furniture was also selected to match the Beaux Arts feel of the building. The main floor reading room, Brett Hall, now has its clerestory windows uncovered to admit more natural light, and its decorative vaulted ceiling is also restored. New reference desks and hand-loomed rugs were also custom designed to match the style of the interior. Light fixtures too were cleaned, restored or replicated. Less visibly, new solutions have been found to accommodate data and power cabling so that the Main Library's computer resources can meet modern needs.

The Louis Stokes Wing is linked to the Main Library by a tunnel running beneath the intervening Eastman Reading Garden. While still respecting the 1903 plan, the new 10-storey wing takes an individualistic approach. In scale it matches the adjacent Federal Reserve Bank, but its oval shape and floor-to-ceiling glazing make the building outward-looking, in contrast to the Main Library, where Brett Hall provides a secluded internal focus. However, many of the colours used in the new wing reflect those of the original. Interior organization also echoes the Main Library's centrally orientated network of departments, freeing up the naturally lit periphery for reading and work areas. There is also provision for comprehensive electronic services, from computerized cataloguing between departments and all other Cleveland libraries, to self-directed services such as searching the Worldwide Web. The final stage of this intelligent and sophisticated renovation will be the upgrading of the Eastman Reading Garden.

Architect: **Hardy Holzman Pfeiffer Associates**.
Commissioning Client: **Cleveland Public Library**. Total Floor Space: **255,000 square feet** (Main Library), **270,000 square feet** (Louis Stokes Wing). Number of Levels: **10** (Louis Stokes Wing). Contract Cost: **US$65.1 million** (Main Library), **US$90 million** (Louis Stokes Wing). Completed: **1997–8**.

right The refurbished Brett Hall in the Main Library.
opposite The map collection on the sixth floor of the new Louis Stokes Wing with ceiling design by Cleveland artist Holly Morrison.
below The site plan shows the relationship of the two buildings; the section demonstrates their relative scale.
overleaf Decorative lending desks in the Louis Stokes Wing.

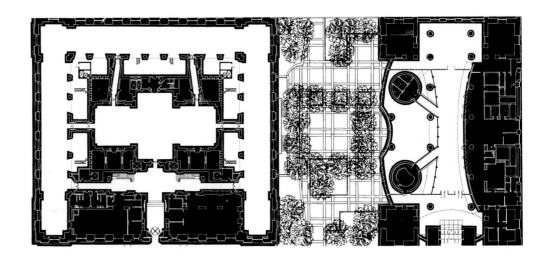

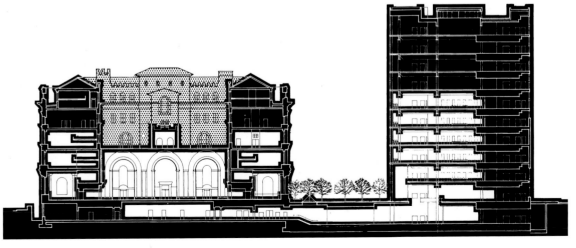

above Spacious reading areas are situated close to windows in the newly built section of the library.
left Playful decorative sculpture adorns a gate in the Eastman Reading Garden which unites the two main elements of the scheme.
opposite An interior view through the Louis Stokes Wing shows the expansive use of Georgian marble.

This is a design scheme that is as much about symbolism as it is space or structure. On the site of the terrible Hanshin-Awaji earthquake of 1994, a Buddhist sect has rebuilt its prayer hall as an offering to heal the physical and psychological wounds inflicted on the area by the disaster. Architect Shin Takamatsu chose to show the positive side of nature: he has created the new building by grouping timber poles made from 16 giant cedar trees, all more than 100 years old, on a mountain site which is sacred to followers of the Buddhist saint Myoken Bosatsu. The cedars form a tower which has a star-shaped floor plan and is topped by a glass element modelled on a pattern of chevrons – the sect's symbol.

The interior of this extraordinary building reflects the idea of 'waiting for something to arise in this world', explains the architect. Thus, an evocative, film-covered glass floor hangs within the space. Beneath, at the base of the tower, are guest rooms. Otherwise areas are not committed to specific functions: worshippers are free to roam within the spectacular geometry of the beams, in keeping with an environmental philosophy more directed towards 'the structure of the mind' than the structure of the building.

This is a project that reaffirms Takamatsu's reputation as a master maker of exceptional interior spaces, one who takes a singular approach to the underlying need for any new facility. In this case, the ecological message about renewal communicated by the cedars inspired him to create a stunning contemporary structure as a sanctum for one of the world's oldest religions.

Designer: **Shin Takamatsu Architect & Associates**.
Commissioning Client: **Kansai Sinnyoji Nose Myoken-zan**. Total Floor Space: **901.5 square metres**.
Number of Levels: **2**. Contract Cost: **US$5 million**.
Completed: **April 1998**.

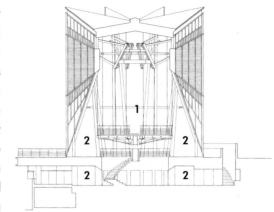

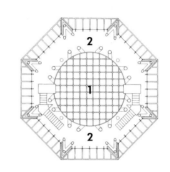

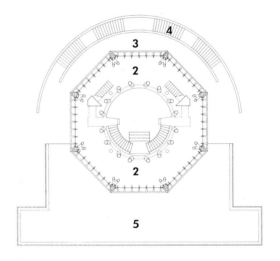

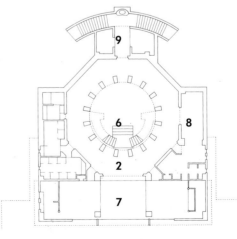

opposite The glass floor which hangs within the interior volume of the Buddhist temple has an otherworldly quality.
right Section and floor plans.

key
1 worship hall
2 corridor
3 passage
4 outside stairs
5 stage
6 entrance hall
7 relaxing room
8 office
9 entrance

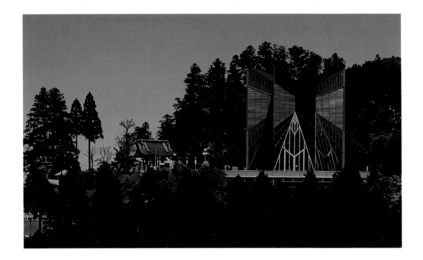

above and below The form of the building with its grouping of cedarwood structural elements suggests rebirth within the landscape.

right The view from the ground floor up through the transparent upper floor reveals breathtaking interior geometries.

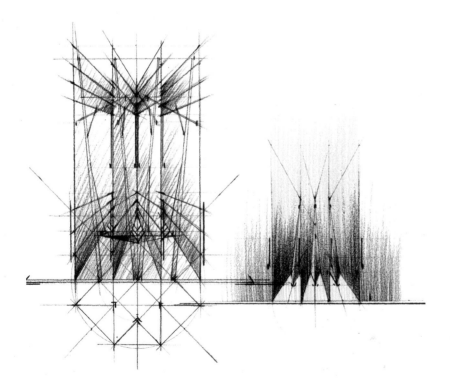

When Behnisch, Sabatke, Behnisch created a new administrative headquarters for the Landesgirokasse, the main Stuttgart clearing bank, the building programme was well advanced before the planners asked the architect to address the problem of an office district that had become lifeless outside of business hours. The decision was made to incorporate street-level public amenities, including a shop, Italian restaurant and three-auditorium art house cinema, when the structural characteristics were already fixed. But it is to Behnisch's credit that the resulting public amenities – and especially the focal-point cinema, the 'Atelier am Bollwerk' – do not appear as an after-thought.

The Bollwerk banking services centre offices sit at upper levels around a courtyard that includes a reflecting pool and a dramatic sloping glass enclosure for the foyer. Within the building shell that already existed, the cinema has been designed in as generous and relaxed a way as possible. The street-level foyer incorporates one of the auditoria and the space is planned as though it were an extension of the street. The fully glazed external façade can be opened up in warm weather and provides a key point of engagement with the outside – an internal space that becomes external, an effect heightened by extending the bold colours of walls and floor coverings to the exterior.

The other two auditoria are located off a courtyard one level below that is accessible via a broad stairway and a second foyer, also marked by intense colour. The interior of each auditorium uses different light effects and wall finishes to establish an individual character while addressing acoustic demands. One cinema uses coloured textile panels in a chess pattern; another features alternating plain and perforated surfaces. The overall result is a trio of highly individual auditoria that were not simply dropped into the confines of a nine-to-five office building but were artfully designed to draw in the public during leisure hours and so provide a social focus for the whole district.

Designer: **Behnisch, Sabatke, Behnisch**. Client: **Kinoverwaltung Erasmus**. Total Floor Space: **1,200 square metres**. Number of Levels: **2**. Contract Cost: **Confidential**. Completed: **June 1997**.

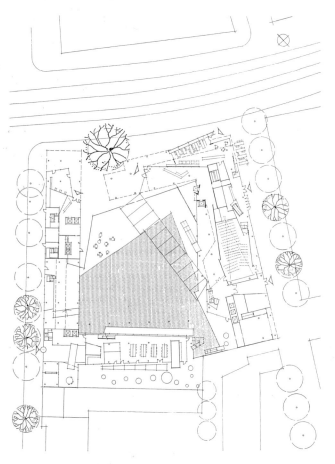

left The site plan shows how the public amenities are grouped around the bank's main office facilities which are located at upper levels.
opposite The bold colours of the cinema entrance are visible through the glazed façade.

opposite Interior detailing pays homage
to Fellini and other film heroes.
below The auditorium extends playfulness
with colour and materials.

4.5 `airport gardermoen` oslo, norway

A new airport on the outskirts of Oslo presented the challenge of building a modern facility that reflected the national identity of a country popularly associated with timber rather than high-tech materials. This sense of national image was a key part of the brief devised by OSL, a company set up to act as a client for this major project. A spirit of accommodation set the tone, with a joint venture, Aviaplan, being created between three architectural practices and a multidisciplinary engineering firm to execute the scheme. The brief identified the spirit of Norway as being best expressed by its perceived virtues: prudence, closeness to nature, openness and a responsible use of natural resources.

The airport comprises a whole range of buildings, including customs headquarters and a railway station. However, the defining building was always going to be Aviaplan's central terminal, which represents a simple conceptual approach. It is essentially a great hall with a roof that sweeps upwards towards a large glazed wall facing the airside – the clearest possible way for the building to mediate between the airborne and the land-bound. Arrivals are at ground level, departures on an upper level that floats within the terminal space. Simple and rational circulation has been devised for arrivals and departures, but it is through the use of materials and sense of internal space that the architects have best succeeded in creating the distinctive sense of calm and clarity that the brief prescribed.

Norwegian wood is visible everywhere in the interior. Check-in desks, floors, bar panelling, ceilings and tall slatted office screens are all timber. In less skilful hands the effect might seem wilfully folksy (a criticism levelled by some at the terminal's timber-laced roof structure, where steel might seem the more 'natural' material to use), but the superior quality of the interior design largely negates such judgments. Despite the enormous internal volumes that confronted the

designers, a wealth of calm surfaces, natural materials and subtle use of light combine to give the heart of Gardermoen airport a sense of distinction and place all too rare in the soulless catalogue of international air passenger processing plants.

Architect: **Aviaplan**. Commissioning Client: **OSL**. Total Floor Space: **136,000 square metres**. Number of Levels: **2**. Contract Cost: **£256 million**. Completed: **1998**.

left The control tower rises above the main terminal building.
opposite A view towards the check-in desks at departure level.
below Cross-section through the contact pier and air bridges and (opposite below) longitudinal section through the terminal hall.

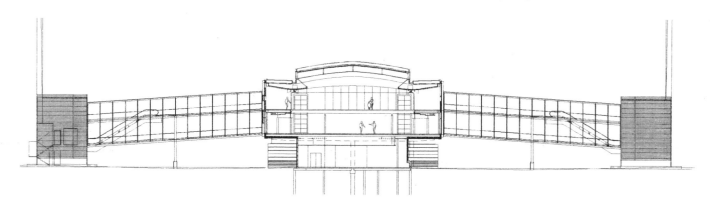

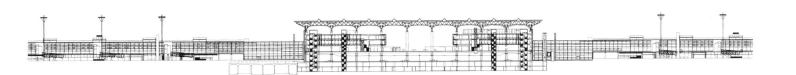

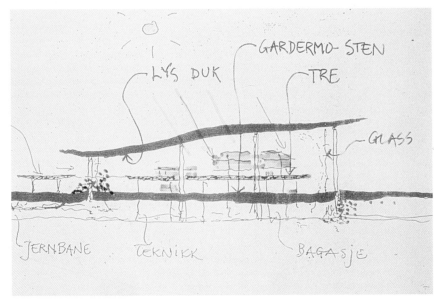

opposite above The projection of Norway's national identity was
instrumental in the decision to use local timber in ceilings.

opposite The sketch shows the form of the building.

above The view down into the restaurant area from the arrivals level.
Again the interior makes extensive use of Norwegian wood.

Hackney in East London is not a district famous for its architecture. The Geffrye Museum (specializing in English furniture and interiors) is the borough's only Grade I-listed building. The original museum is a conversion of some early eighteenth-century almshouses elegantly built in Queen Anne style and enclosing three sides of a garden. The new extension by Branson Coates is an uncompromising contemporary design linked to the original museum's south and rear corner and providing a new mix of gallery and education space as well as a restaurant and retail centre. Overall, the interior adheres to a domestic architectural scale entirely appropriate to the nature of the institution.

The extension is a two-storey, horseshoe-shaped brick building that is visually distinct from the rectilinear original and attached by means of a ramp and a low, undulating steel, copper and glass roof which, according to architect Nigel Coates, fits 'like a hand in a glove'. There is no direct entrance to the extension; its complementary nature is stressed by the fact that visitors must enter it from the interior of the original museum.

The first space in the extension is the restaurant with views over the rear gardens. Otherwise the ground floor is almost entirely devoted to a gallery showing English domestic interiors throughout the twentieth century. This section brings the Geffrye's period rooms up to date. A dramatic curving concrete staircase with steel and glass balustrades leads to a lower concourse containing a temporary exhibition gallery, two large rooms dedicated to educational activities and a design centre for the display of craft objects and furniture made in East London. The extension is also designed to meet stringent environmental standards necessary to conserve old furniture without the need for air-conditioning. The external walls are substantial enough to absorb changes in air temperature and humidity; the roof is heavily insulated and the lower-ground-floor windows are shaded with a brise-soleil.

Designer: **Branson Coates Architecture**. Commissioning Client: **The Geffrye Museum**. Total Floor Space: **1,900 square metres**. Number of Levels: **2**. Contract Cost: **£3.2 million**. Completed: **November 1998**.

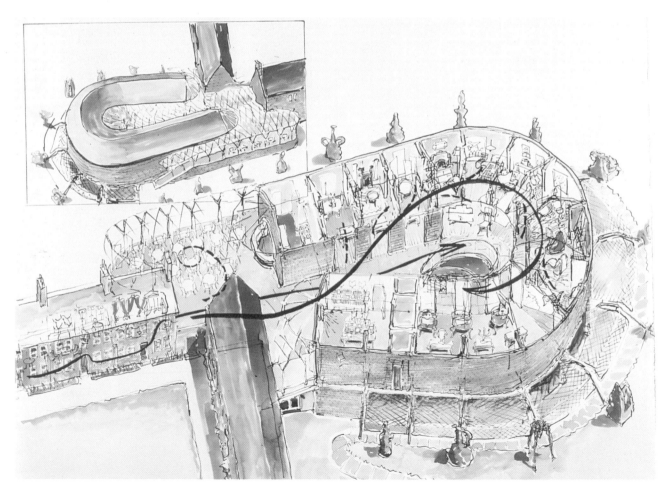

opposite Branson Coates' sketch shows the horseshoe-shaped
extension in relation to the original museum.

above and overleaf right The dramatic staircase feature
which links the two levels of the new Geffrye extension, a
curvaceous configuration of concrete, glass, steel and wood.

right Ground-floor plan.
below right Lower concourse plan.
bottom The sections show the integration of the new wing into the existing building.
below Exterior view of the brick horseshoe which respects its historic context while retaining an essentially contemporary presence.

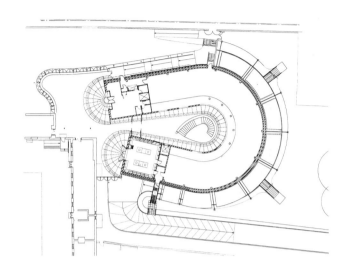

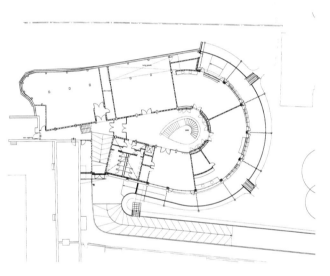

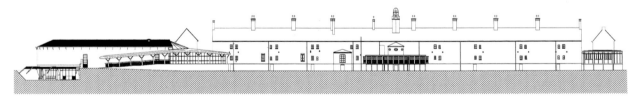

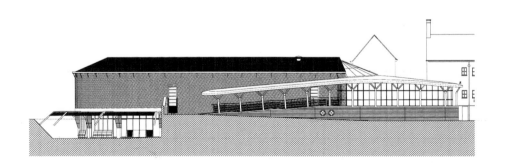

When the German Federal Parliament, the Bundestag, decided to relocate from Bonn to Berlin to reoccupy the historic Reichstag in the heady atmosphere following reunification, the project to restore the building highlighted that special interdependence between politics and architecture. Following a competition in 1992, Foster and Partners was appointed to design a scheme with four key objectives: first, to create one of the world's great democratic forums; second, to make the process of government more publicly accessible; third, to reflect an understanding of history; and fourth, to promote an environment-friendly agenda.

Damaged by war and insensitive rebuilding, the fabric of the old Reichstag was peeled back to reveal charred timbers and Soviet occupation graffiti as testament to the troubled history of Germany in the twentieth century. These historic elements have been integrated into the newly converted building, and its giant masonry shell opened up to natural light and public views through a series of glazed interventions reflecting the transparency of democracy. Junctions between the new and existing fabric are clearly expressed, making the Reichstag an updated text that can be 'read' by the visitor.

The building's original entrance from the west has been reinstated, with a grand flight of stairs leading to the principal parliament level on the first floor and to a sucession of other working levels. Above them, the public realm reasserts itself in a roof terrace that gives visitors access to a restaurant and to a dome within which twin helical ramps lead to an elevated observation platform. The symbolism of the people rising above the heads of their political leaders is not lost within the technical ingenuity of this cupola, which has a mirrored cone at its core to reflect light into the main chamber.

Much has been made of the Reichstag's green credentials – its radical power system uses eco-fuels such as vegetable oils – and of the appointment of a British architect to lead the conversion. But the principal collaborator on the interiors was Danish graphic artist Per Arnoldi, who was instrumental in the choice of dynamic primary colours such as deep French blues, sunflower yellows and bright reds for 19 large public rooms. This approach was in response to complaints by Chancellor Kohl that the architectural profession was 'obsessed with grey'. These colour splashes counterpoint the quiet presence of new stone floors and help to moderate the monumental character of a building which conducts a welcome dialogue between past and present.

Designer: **Foster and Partners**. Commissioning Client: **German Federal Parliament**. Total Floor Space: **61,166 square metres**. Number of Levels: **6 plus dome**. Contract Cost: **DM 600 million**. Completed: **April 1999**.

below Cross-section of the Plenary building in the converted Reichstag.
opposite Looking down from the base of the dome into the main chamber.
overleaf Inside the main chamber which is dominated by the eagle symbol and (right) inside the dome, which has a giant mirrored cone to reflect light down into the chamber.

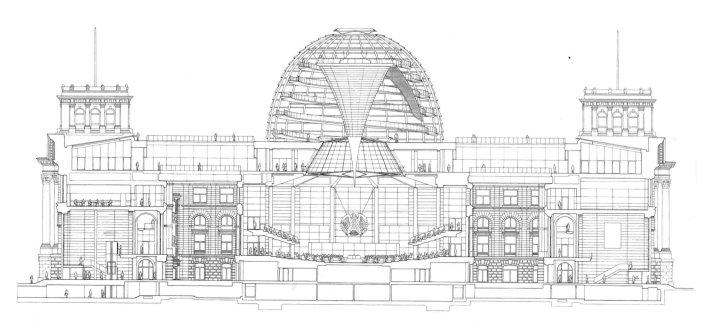

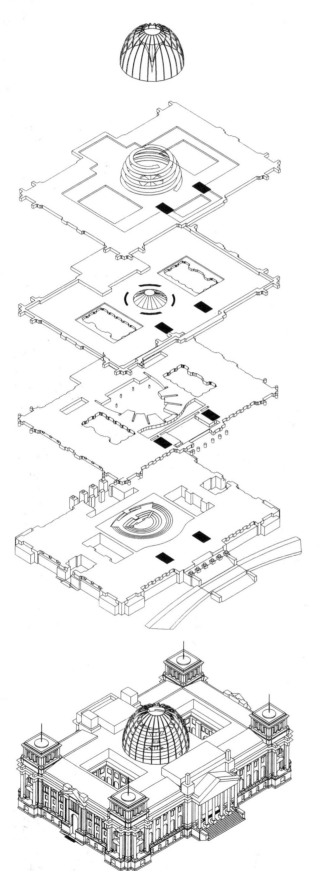

far left Exploded plans and axonometric of the politically sensitive Reichstag project.
above Conceptual sketch by Sir Norman Foster.
left Exterior view showing the cupola and part of the roof terrace.
top The observation deck at the base of the cupola symbolically lifting the people above the politicians.
opposite The Reichstag interior retains war damage and grafitti as evocative reminders of the building's history.

American architect Steven Holl is in good company with his new Helsinki contemporary art museum. Kiasma's neighbours include Eliel Saarinen's Helsinki Station to the east and Alvar Aalto's Finlandia Hall to the north. The building is next door to the new £100-million Finnish National Opera House and is intended to form part of a 'culture mile' stretching along the shoreline of Töölönlahti Lake. Perhaps the modernist authority and intricacy of the urban context explains Holl's almost surgical approach to the museum's design. Kiasma derives its name from 'chiasma', the term for the crossover of chromosones in genetics, and the museum's interior galleries derive their unusual spatial qualities from a bold and inventive crossover of architectural elements.

Holl's competition-winning scheme involved the penetration of a rectangular block by a structure with a glass and concrete façade that curves through the main building, becoming its backbone. The result is a highly expressive but nevertheless disciplined sequence of 25 organically formed internal galleries – each a semi-rectangle with one curved wall. The slight irregularity of the design adds intrigue to the austere intensity of the spaces so that the visitor is confronted with a continuously changing perspective. Contemporary works are presented on large expanses of exposed concrete that is subtly grazed with natural and artificial light, giving it a handcrafted feel. This surface deliberately contrasts with the industrial finish of the zinc, aluminium and glass exterior.

In a climate of winter darkness and intense summer sun, Holl's building is careful to mediate the relationship between natural and artificial light. The curved roof section has 'bowtie' skylights which distribute light into the building, as does the curved 'wall of ice'. Some of the rooms, however, are entirely enclosed and illuminated by fluorescent lights installed in ceiling pockets and by special low-voltage Erco Quinta spotlights. L'Observatoire International, the lighting consultant on the project, were part of a multinational team that ensured Holl's scheme could employ the most advanced technology while respecting the unique national heritage of Finnish modernism. Kiasma is a distinguished newcomer to Helsinki, and in its graceful interweaving of space and light it need feel no inferiority complex about its modern credentials. Designer: **Steven Holl Architects**. Commissioning Client: **Finnish Ministry of Education**. Total Floor Space: **12,000 square metres**. Number of Levels: **5**. Contract Cost: **Confidential**. Completed: **May 1998**.

above The exterior view shows the penetration of the rectangular block by the curved structure that forms its spine.
right The section shows the gallery space within the curved wall.
opposite Interior view of the sculptural public walkway.

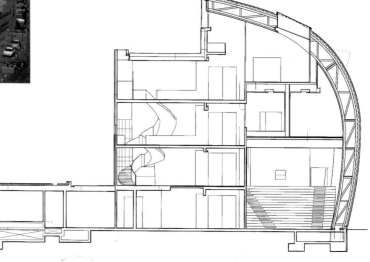

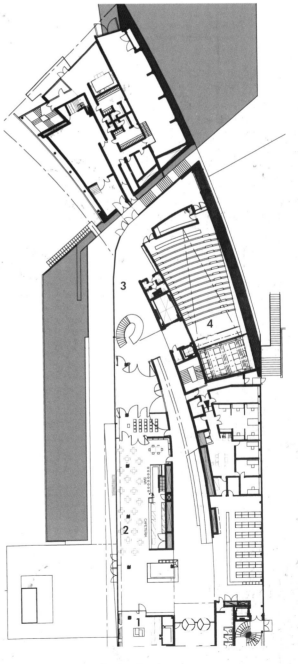

opposite Interior views of the organic gallery and public spaces reflecting the designer's confident response to Helsinki's modernist heritage.

above A watercolour rendering by Steven Holl.

right The first-floor plan.

key
1 book store
2 cafeteria
3 auditorium lobby
4 auditorium

4.9 brooklyn academy of music rose cinemas brooklyn, new york, usa

Opened in 1861, the Brooklyn Academy of Music (BAM) is America's oldest performing arts centre. Its original central feature, a concert hall, once attracted performers like Sarah Bernhardt and Enrico Caruso. Today BAM operates as a vigorous contemporary cultural centre providing a cornerstone for the revitalization of downtown Brooklyn. However, the centre's own needs have changed considerably over the years and this was the basis for commissioning architects Hardy Holzman Pfeiffer Associates (HHPA) to undertake a bold reconfiguration of its facilities.

Central to the HHPA solution was a change of focus for an internal area known as the Lepercq Space. HHPA added a new café here, and made this the primary lobby space on the first floor (second floor, US) through the introduction of a new escalator connection. A second and more radical change came with the decision to convert the ornate Helen Carey Playhouse into four cinema auditoria, the Rose Cinemas. The prospect of 'multiplexing' an historic auditorium met with resistance in some quarters, but in fact the Playhouse had long been an impractical asset. Built as a concert hall, it had inadequate fly space and stage depth for most types of live performances. With the adjacent Opera House being the preferred venue for many live events, the Helen Carey Playhouse could be used to provide a venue for BAM's expansion into independent film exhibition.

The new auditoria are small, shaped volumes set within the larger enclosure of the existing historic playhouse. Two are at street level (with 111 and 156 seats respectively), and two larger ones (300 and 216 seats) at mezzanine level. The architectural significance of the original auditorium was retained by preserving its most distinctive features and making them powerful elements within the new scheme. In this way part of an ornate plaster proscenium arch is pressed into service in one auditorium. Coffered ceilings are retained, as is an existing inner lobby area with arched entry vaults. Seating, however, makes no concession to historicism with a multi-coloured treatment that resembles a cheerful scattering of confectionery – all part of an inventive scheme that took four years to complete.

Architect: **Hardy Holzman Pfeiffer Associates**.
Commissioning Client: **Brooklyn Academy of Music**.
Total Floor Space: **30,000 square feet**. Number of Levels:
2. Contract Cost: **US$10 million**. Completed: **1998**.

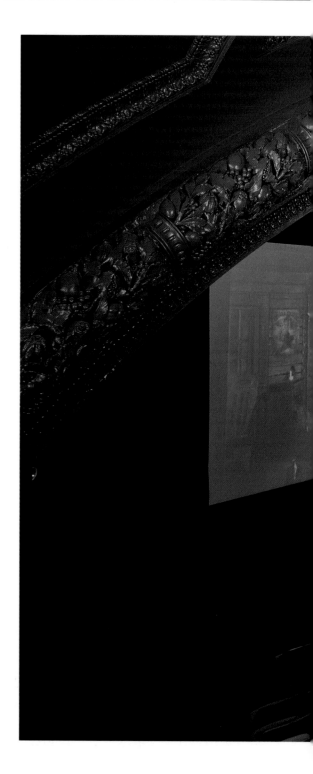

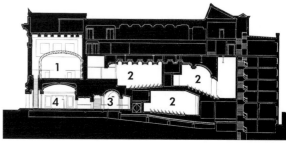

above One of the four new cinema interiors skilfully created within the ornate frame of a famous historic playhouse.

Cross-section
1 Lepercq Space
2 cinema
3 promenade
4 main lobby

Mezzanine-level

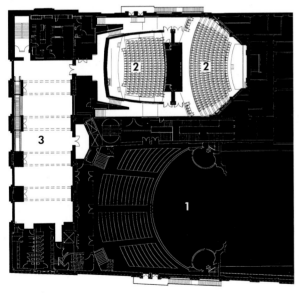

key
1 Opera House
2 cinema
3 Lepercq Space

Orchestra-level

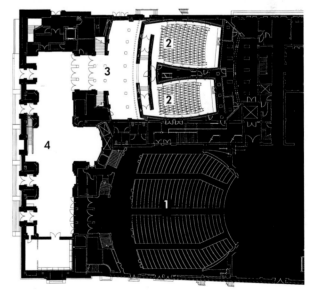

key
1 Opera House
2 cinema
3 promenade
4 main lobby

opposite and top Interior views of the spectacular lighting in the
Lepercq Space; old showbiz themes never fade.

With three main structures and a total area of three million square feet, Kuala Lumpur International Airport is a facility for the next generation of air travel. Its architectural design was driven by Japanese architect Kisho Kurokawa, but the whole project involved an alliance between architect and mechanical and civil engineers, as well as landscape and signage designers. British design firm BDG McColl were responsible for overseeing all internal areas, including retail, concessions, check-in desks and VIP lounges; they also controlled much of the detail within the main terminal and the contact pier. The third structure in the complex is a satellite building.

The dominant design impact of such a major complex derives not from the detail but from the grand iconography of the infrastructure. Kurokawa's scheme uses a bold mixture of distinctive Malaysian design modified by the lineaments of state-of-the-art building technology. Avoiding the literal, Kurokawa has instead created an interplay of near-abstract shapes that manages to suggest traditional local architecture as well as the language of modern multinational aeronautical design. Dramatically tapered roof supports are openly suggestive of Islamic columns. Meanwhile, the stainless-steel roof forms of the main terminal clearly refer to the sinuous lines of aircraft.

Another important design element is the expression of the airport's environmental aspirations. The complex was sited in a cleared forest, and parts of the forest have been incorporated into the airport. The central orientation point of the satellite building is a spectacular landscaped courtyard, and this finds an echo on the landside of the main terminal where another landscaped area links the grand building to its natural surroundings. The airside of the terminal, meanwhile, celebrates technology in a spectacular glazed curtain wall joining it to the contact pier. The traditional and the futuristic have been blended together in an airport that is as accomplished in its interior problem-solving as it is in its masterplanning.

Architectural Design: **Kisho Kurokawa Architect & Associates**. Project architect: **Malaysian Japanese Airport Consortium**. Collaborating Designers: **BDG McColl**. Commissioning Client: **Kuala Lumpur International Airport Berhad**. Total Floor Space: **170,640 square metres** (Terminal Building), **92,400 square metres** (Contact Pier), **142,890 square metres** (Satellite Building). Number of Levels: **6** (Terminal Building); **4** (Contact Pier); **4** (Satellite Building). Interior Contract Cost: **£2 million**. Completed: **1998**.

below The airport masterplan by Kisho Kurokawa in association with Akitek Jururancang, Malaysia.
opposite Passenger concourse in the contact pier.
overleaf Interior views reflect the blend of modern international airport design with local architectural traditions. The dramatically tapered roof supports suggest Islamic columns.

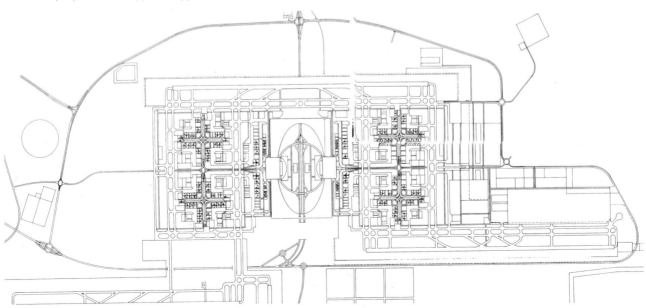

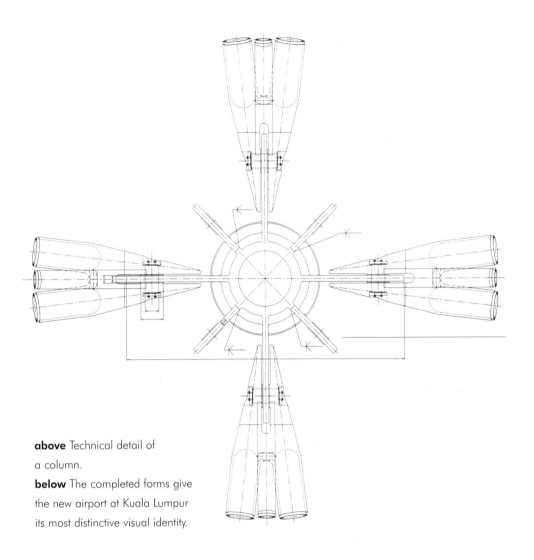

above Technical detail of
a column.
below The completed forms give
the new airport at Kuala Lumpur
its most distinctive visual identity.

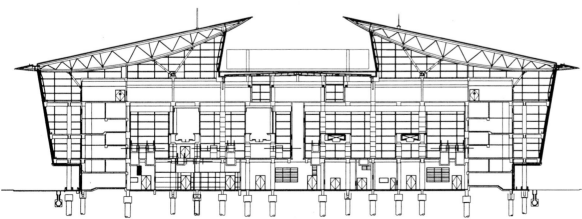

above Passenger areas
designed to provide a
sense of place and space.
left Section through the
contact pier.

Munich's Salvatorschule is a famous late-nineteenth century building in neo-Renaissance style that latterly housed a covered market in its ground floor. World War Two bomb damage had claimed the building's top storey and subsequently a shallow hipped roof was built in its place to protect the surviving two storeys and basement. The Salvatorschule's recent conversion into a Literaturhaus – an increasingly popular type of German institution dedicated to literary readings and events – is an object lesson in how to reconcile past and present with great economy and logic.

Designers Kiessler+Partner decided to draw a clear line between the new and old structures. The missing third storey was reinstated using light concrete slabs supporting

steel and glass walls. This created an independent modern component that approximates the original contours of the upper building despite having the look of a temporary cube structure. Visually, this treatment presents an honest approach to the 'extension' but it was also determined by practical considerations: the brittle brickwork below could only support a relatively lightweight addition.

The new top floor contains three halls for public events, offering magnificent city views, and the internal spaces have a clean, uncluttered look that carries through the light visual lines of the exterior. In doing so, it emulates the pattern of the historic structure in which the façade's bold arches are repeated throughout the interior. Below, the renovation responds well to the neo-Renaissance style of the original building with offices, a library, and a literary café on the ground floor. Installations by New York artist Jenny Holzer reinforce the interior's preoccupation with bringing contemporary culture to Munich's traditional inner city.

Designer: **Kiessler+Partner Architects**. Commissioning Client: **Stiftung Buch Media and Literature Foundation**. Total Floor Space: **4,013 square metres**. Number of Levels: **1**. Contract Cost: **£6 million**. Completed: **Spring 1997**.

opposite below and left Exterior views of Munich's Literaturhaus reveal the modern third-storey extension to the building.
below Ground-floor plan.

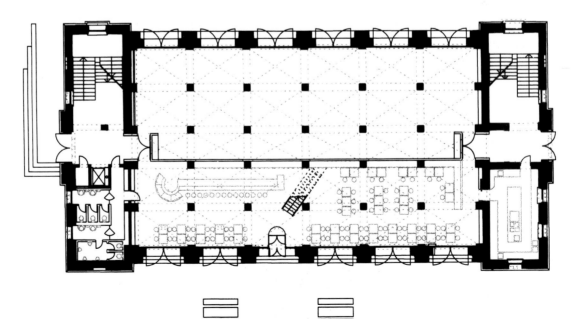

above Inside the new concrete, steel and glass top floor, designed with three spaces for public events.

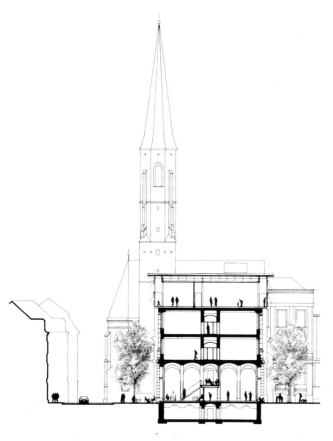

left The cross-section shows the working of the building into Munich's historic inner city.
below The restored ground-floor public spaces reserve the neo-Renaissance flavour.

above The lightweight top-floor extension offers magnificent views of the city.
right The auditorium, part of an arts facility that enhances Munich's cultural life.

Sited in splendid isolation close to the remote New Mexico town of Ruidoso, this unusual theatre by Antoine Predock takes its form from the spectacular landscape in which it sits, particularly the Sierra Blanca (white mountains) to the west. The building is a sculpted limestone mass, against which is butted a light-refracting steel-and-glass element. The juxtaposition of the monolithic mother ship, hewn as if from stone, with its light and fragile lobby is part of a deliberate composition by the architect. Not only does the theatre maximize its dramatic location, but it also avoids the blunt, fly-tower form typical of its type by integrating back-of-house facilities for touring shows into a streamlined design.

The entry lobby and gathering space, which consciously subverts the mass of the building, is the scheme's most distinctive interior. As you step up from the desert plain, beginning an ascent into the auditorium, its faceted and partially fritted glass elements create shimmering geometries on the limestone floors and walls. Laminated cracked glass

balustrading on the staircase continues this theme, as do the cracked glass panels which provide a measure of privacy in an upper-level theatre club.

The auditorium itself, scaled down during development from 800 seats to 514, is an intimate space with the audience pulled as close to the stage as possible in 'finger balconies' that wrap around the room. A series of drapes and partitions in the backstage area can alter the acoustics of the peforming space. The Spencer Theater owes its existence to local New Mexico resident Jackie Spencer, who had the vision for the venue, raised the money and contacted Antoine Predock. The result is a public arts building in which the setting, structure and staging form a satisfying theatrical whole.

Designer: **Antoine Predock Architects**. Commissioning Client: **Spencer Theater**. Total Floor Space: **52,000 square feet**. Number of Levels: **2**. Contract Cost: **US$17 million**. Completed: **October 1997**.

below Ground-floor and first-floor (second, US) plans

key
1 lobby
2 ticket office
3 auditorium
4 stage house
5 shop
6 courtyard
7 offices
8 terraces

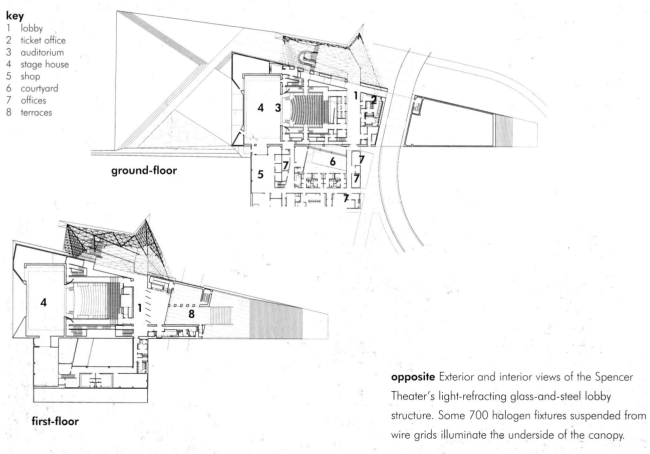

ground-floor

first-floor

opposite Exterior and interior views of the Spencer Theater's light-refracting glass-and-steel lobby structure. Some 700 halogen fixtures suspended from wire grids illuminate the underside of the canopy.

left The idea of the theatre being created by a fissure in the landscape is expressed by interior panels of fritted and cracked glass on the main stairwell.
above A view of the café terrace with coloured-glass ceiling sculptures by artist Dale Chihuly. The high-altitude location means the space remains relatively cool in summer.

Allford Hall Monaghan Morris
2nd Floor, Blocks 5–23, Old Street, London
EC1V 9HL, UK

Allford Hall Monaghan Morris was founded in
London in 1989, the partners having studied and
worked together for five years previously. The
practice specializes in educational, health,
transport, leisure and residential schemes. Current
large-scale projects include competition-winning
designs for a bus station, a theatre, an art gallery
and a primary school. The office is also involved in
an international touring exhibition for Millennium
Products, a housing project for the Joseph
Rowntree Foundation in Birmingham, an
apartment block for the Peabody Trust in London,
a large private house in Kenwood and three office
buildings in Central London. The partners teach at
the Bartlett School of Architecture and have
lectured extensively in the UK and abroad.

Anderson Architects
55 Vandam Street, New York, NY 10013, USA

Anderson Architects specializes in architecture,
urban design and interior space planning. The
company was founded by Ross Anderson who
received his Masters degree in Architecture from
Harvard University and his undergraduate degree
from Stanford University. Prior to forming his own
practice he worked as partner with Frederic
Schwartz in the design consultancy
Anderson/Schwartz architects. He has taught at
Yale, Columbia, Carnegie-Mellon and Parsons
School of Design. Anderson Architects has been
voted one of the top 100 design firms in the world
by both *Architectural Digest* and *Metropolitan
Home* magazines and has also been awarded an
ID Magazine Gold Medal for office environments.
In 1997 Ross Anderson was recipient of the
prestigious Rome Prize in Architecture. Recent
interior design projects include salons, studio and
office for Bumble & Bumble hairdressers in New
York, educational classroom and lab facilities for
Friends Seminary, also in New York, and a winery
production facility in Ravenswood, California.

Apicella Associates (now Pentagram)
11 Needham Road, London W11 2RP, UK

Lorenzo Apicella was born in Ravello, Italy, in
1957. He studied at Nottingham University and
Canterbury College of Art and the Royal College
of Art in London, graduating in 1981. He worked
for Skidmore Owings & Merrill in Houston, Texas,
at CZWG and as Head of Architecture and Design
at Imagination Design & Communications in
London. He founded Apicella Associates in 1988
working on masterplanning, large-scale
exhibitions and interiors, such as the second-floor
restaurant at Oxo Tower Wharf in London. Clients
included the Foreign and Commonwealth Office,
Philips Electronics, Spectrum Communications,
Volvo, La Perla, Docklands Development
Corporation and Virgin Atlantic. Since 1983 he
has been a member of RIBA, for whom he has
chaired regional juries. In 1993 he was invited to
judge the American Institute of Architects Awards
for Southern California in San Diego. Apicella is
currently a visiting lecturer at the Graduate School
of Architecture at Oxford Brookes University and
external examiner for the School of Design at UCE
Birmingham. He is a Fellow of both the Chartered
Society of Designers and the Royal Society of Arts.

In 1998 Lorenzo joined Pentagram Design in
London as a partner.

Aviaplan As
Uranienborgvn 11, Postboks 7057, Majorstua
0306, Oslo, Norway

Aviaplan comprises six Scandinavian partner
companies, Narud-Stokke-Wiig, Architects and
Planners; Niels Torp AS, Architects and Designers;
Skaarup & Jespersen, Architects and Planners;
Calvert & Clark Architects; Bjorbekk & Lindheim
AS, Landscape Architects; and Hjellnes Cowias
Consulting Engineers and Planners. The group
was founded in 1989 since which time they have
worked on projects connected to the new
international airport in Oslo as well as other
schemes related to buildings, industrial
developments and infrastructural development.

BDG McColl
24 St John Street, London EC1M 4AY, UK

BDG McColl (formerly the Business Design Group)
was founded in 1962. Specializing in office
planning and design, they have offices throughout
the UK and in Frankfurt and Budapest. Clients BDP
have worked with include Thomas Cook, American
Express, the British Inland Revenue, Department of
Trade and Industry, Department of the Environment
and Department of Transport, British Gas, Ernst
and Young, Smith Kline Beecham and BZW. The
practice is split into four sectors each catering to
different areas of the marketplace. BDG McColl
Architecture deals with the design of shopping
centres, offices and manufacturing facilities; BDG
McColl Communications with graphic design and
brand identities as well as staff communications;
BDG McColl Retail and Leisure with the
development of brand strategy and the design of
retail and leisure environments; and BDG McColl
Workplace offers a service in the space-planning,
design and construction management of
workplace environments. Recent projects include
Waterstone's, Glasgow; South Village at the
Bluewater development in Kent; a shopping centre
in Exeter; Barclays Bank in Newark; the Arthur
Andersen Business Consulting offices in London
and the British Council in Mexico.

BDP – Building Design Partnership
PO Box 4WD, 16 Gresse Street, London
W1A 4WD, UK

BDP was established in 1961 as an interior,
graphic and design group specializing in space-
planning, workplace design and retail design
working both in the UK and abroad.
Recent/current projects include the interiors of the
Adam Opel headquarters at Russelsheim near
Frankfurt; the University of Sunderland, fitouts for
British Telecom, the Prudential and Halifax, as well
as retail interiors in Germany, Portugal and Spain.

Behnisch, Sabatke, Behnisch
Büro Sillenbuch, Gorch-Fock-Strasse 30,
70619, Stuttgart, Germany

Günter Behnisch was born in Dresden in 1922.
He studied at the Technical University of Stuttgart
and set up his own office in 1952. In 1979 he
founded Behnisch & Partner with Winfried Buxel,
Manfred Sabatke and Erhard Tranker. Today the
firm has two offices, Behnisch & Partner and

Behnisch, Sabatke, Behnisch and has taken on
two further partners, Stefan Behnisch and Günther
Schaller. Both practices concentrate on large-scale
public commissions. Recent projects include
banks in Frankfurt, Munich and Stuttgart; schools'
sports facilities, and the German Flight Safety
Bureau. Günter Behnisch is a member of the
Akademie der Kunste, an Honorary Doctor at the
University of Stuttgart, a member of the
International Academy of Architecture in Sofia and
an honorary member of the Royal Incorporation of
Architects in Scotland. In 1992 he was awarded
the Gold Medal by the Architecture Academy
in Paris.

BOA (Barber Osgerby Associates)
Studio 8, Turnham Green Terrace Mews, London
W14 1QU, UK

BOA was founded in 1996 by Edward Barber and
Jay Osgerby who met when they were studying
together at the Royal College of Art, London. The
practice has designed interiors for residential and
commercial premises and has had furniture
manufactured by Cappellini and the Conran
shops. Its latest project is the Soho Brewing
Company – a micro-brewery and restaurant in
London. It received the award for Best New
Designer in 1998 at the International
Contemporary Furniture Fair in New York. Recent
projects include a pharmacy and herbal
apothecary interior and a flagship hair salon for
Trevor Sorbie.

Abe Bonnema
Bureau for Architecture and Environmental
Planning BV, Postbus 15, 9254 ZV Hardgarijp,
The Netherlands

Abe Bonnema's earliest designs are to be found in
Leeuwarden and include the Girobank Building,
offices for the municipal social services and for the
insurance companies Avero and FBTO. He is best
known for his design of the head office of the
Nationale Nederlanden in Rotterdam which, at
150 metres high, is the tallest building in The
Netherlands.

Branson Coates Architecture Ltd
23 Old Street, London EC1V 9RR, UK

Branson Coates was founded in 1985 by Nigel
Coates and Doug Branson. Nigel Coates was
born in 1949 and attended the Architectural
Association where he was Unit Master from 1979
to 1989. In 1983 he formed NATO (Narrative
Architecture Today) with colleagues from the AA.
Doug Branson graduated from the Architectural
Association in 1975, after which he worked with
DEGW. Before he co-founded Branson Coates he
worked in the Branson Helsel Partnership. BCA's
early projects include the Caffe Bongo at Parco in
Tokyo, as well as retail outlets for Katharine
Hamnett, Jigsaw and Jasper Conran. Its work for
these clients continues but more recent schemes
also include the Silo Art Gallery building in Tokyo;
the Nautilus and La Forêt restaurants at Schiphol
Airport, the Geffrye Museum extension in London
and the National Centre for Popular Music in
Sheffield. It was responsible for the Body Zone at
the Millennium Dome in Greenwich and won a
bid for a turnkey commission to provide a
temporary building and exhibition for the
Department of Trade and Industry on Horse

Guards Parade – Powerhouse::uk. Branson Coates has designed numerous exhibitions such as the 'Living Bridges' at the Royal Academy of Arts, London and the 'ecstacity' exhibition at the Design Museum. Nigel Coates is also involved in furniture design and is Professor of Architectural Design at the Royal College of Art, London.

Antonio Citterio and Partners
Via Lovanio 8, 20121 Milan, Italy

Antonio Citterio was born in Meda, Italy, in 1950 and has been involved in industrial and furniture design since 1967. He studied at Milan Polytechnic and in 1973 set up a studio with Paolo Nava. The two have worked jointly and individually for B&B Italia and Flexform among other clients, and in 1979 they were awarded the Compasso d'Oro. In 1987 Terry Dwan became a partner in Studio Citterio Dwan, and the company has undertaken many interior design projects since then, including a range of schemes for Esprit and offices and showrooms for Vitra. Among the work realized in Japan, in partnership with Toshiyuki Kita, is the headquarters in Kobe for World Company; the Corrente Building in Tokyo; and in 1992, the Daigo Headquarters in Tokyo. Recent schemes include stores for Habitat, Cerruti and Arclinea and the interior concept and design for smart car centres for Daimler Chrysler AG. As well as interior design, Citterio continues his interest in product design producing work for Maxalto, Vitra, Arclinea and Flexform. Citterio has taught at the Domus Academy in Milan, at La Spienza University in Rome and has been the external examiner for the Furniture Design Course of the Royal College of Art, London. He has participated in many exhibitions, including independent shows in Hanover, Rome, Amsterdam, Paris and Weil. In 1993 he designed the layout of the exhibition 'Antonio Citterio and Terry Dwan' promoted by Arc en Rêve in Bordeaux which travelled to Osaka and Tokyo in 1994.

Victor López Cotelo Arquitecto
Pasaje de Doña Carlota 8, Madrid, Spain

Victor López Cotelo was born in Madrid in 1947. He studied architecture at the Escuela Técnica Superior de Arquitectura in Madrid and then worked in Munich for a couple of years before starting his collaboration with Studio Alejandro de la Sota. In 1979 he left in order to found his own practice. He has been the recipient of many major national awards, including the COAM prize for government buildings in Valdelaguna, Madrid; first prize in the competition for the restoration of the Palacio de Linares, and the FIBES prize for his work on the Public Library of Salamanca in La Casa de las Conchas. In 1997 he was a finalist in the Spanish Architecture Biennial and the following year his proposal for the School of Architecture in Granada came first in a major international competition. Cotelo has been professor of architecture at the ETSA in Madrid and was also guest professor at the School of Architecture in Munich. His work has been the object of numerous national and international exhibitions and has been published widely throughout the world.

CZWG
17 Bowling Green Lane, London EC1R OQB

CZWG was founded by Nicholas Campbell, Roger Zogolovitch, Rex Wilkinson and Piers Gough who trained together at the Architectural Association in the late 1960s. The company began by transforming existing buildings but now undertakes new-build commissions specializing in innovative private housing. Today it covers a wide spectrum of building types in the public and private sectors, and projects range from urban regeneration and masterplanning to exhibition design. Schemes include the National Gallery Extension, London; the National Portrait Gallery, London; the Leonardo Centre, Uppingham, Rutland; Janet Street-Porter's House, Smithfield, London, and China Wharf Bermondsey, also in London. In 1998 Piers Gough was appointed CBE for services to architecture .

Paul Daly Design Studio and Workshop
11 Hoxton Square, London N1 6NU

Paul Daly was born in Dublin in 1963. He trained at the National College of Art in Dublin and at Goldsmiths College, London, then moved to New York and worked with artists and sculptors as well as with the design group Clodagh and architect Robert Pierpont. He returned to London in 1989 and set up his own design and sculpture studio. From 1991 Daly developed his interest in interior design, creating the Interim Art Gallery in London, the Ri-Ra Club, the Ted Baker shop, the Elbow Room bar and Ozwald Boateng's fashion showroom in Savile Row. Since 1991 Daly has been working on restaurants in London, Newcastle and Leeds. He continues to produce new furniture lines and also collaborates with the band U2, most recently on their 1997–8 'Pop Mart' tour.

Arthur de Mattos Casas
Owen & Mandolfo
192 Lexington Street, New York, NY 10012, USA

Arthur de Mattos Casas was educated at the School of Architecture and Urban Planning, Mackenzie University, São Paulo, Brazil. Additional studies were undertaken both in the United States and Europe. As well as being an associated architect with Owen & Mandolfo, New York, he has an independent architectural practice in São Paulo. He has designed furniture for Arredamento, Teperman and Montenapoleone, as well as for his own showroom, Casas Design. Many of de Mattos Casas' designs have received awards and his work has been published in newspapers and magazines in Brazil, Italy and the United States.

Dempster Thrussel and Rae
DTR Sheard Walshaw, Alberton House; St. Mary's Parsonage, Manchester M3 2WJ, UK

Dempster Thrussell and Rae was formed in January 1992 in Bradford and a branch opened in Manchester the following year. In 1997 the company merged with Sheard Walshaw Partnership creating DTR Sheard Walshaw and a further office was set up in Leeds. Today the practice is involved in architecture, interior and graphic design.

Design Associates
Winterstrasse 4, 81543 Munich, Germany

Design Associates was founded by Uwe Binnberg and Stephan Lang in 1993. Binnberg worked for Frederic Fischer in Los Angeles and Warner Brothers Filmpark where he was involved in the design of science fiction scenarios. Lang collaborated with Skidmore Owings and Merrill, Steidle and Partners and Architekturbüro Strehle in Munich. From 1992 to 1995 he was assistant to Professor Hughes in Munich. Design Associates specializes in product design and furniture prototypes as well as the design of office spaces, shops, sound studios and small-scale architectural projects. They are currently working on a four-storey office building for the insurance company Arag in Munich.

Rena Dumas Architecture Intérieure
5 rue de Mail, 75002, Paris, France

Rena Dumas was born in Greece in 1937. She studied at the Ecole Nationale Superieure des Metiers d'Art in Paris receiving her diploma in 1961. She worked in the Robert Anxionnat studio before founding her own studio (RDAI) in 1970. She specializes in the design of retail outlets and leisure facilities and her clients include Hermès, Charles Jourdan and John Lobb. As well as working in interior design she is also involved in furniture design and has exhibited in Greece, France and Germany. In 1988 she received the Carte Blanche award from the Association for the Enhanced Value of Innovation in Furniture (VIA) for her *Okeanis* collection.

Esherick Homsey Dodge and Davis Architecture and Planning
West Randolph Street, Chicago, IL 60606, USA

Joseph Esherick founded his own practice in 1946 and expanded to include associates George Homsey, Peter Dodge and Charles Davis in 1963; they became partners in 1972. Charles Davis FAIA is the current Senior Design Principal of EHDD. He studied Architecture and Design Administration at the University of California, Berkeley, is the director of the San Francisco chapter of the American Institute of Architects and has taught at the University of Hawaii and UC Berkeley. Today the company has grown substantially in size and scope and has added four principals: Joram Altman, Jim Hastings, Ed Rubin and Blair Spangler. Early work was mainly residential projects in the San Francisco Bay Area but by the late 1960s more complex schemes were being undertaken, including one of the earliest urban shopping complexes, The Cannery, San Francisco. During the 1970s EHDD's work included Bay Area Rapid Transit stations and the award-winning Garfield School, San Francisco. The company's present involvement in aquarium design evolved from the Monterey Bay Aquarium, one of the most widely acclaimed and visited facilities of its kind in the USA. Another area of expertise is the design of university libraries, including the University of California, Santa Cruz Science Library for which it was awarded the Library Building Award in 1993. Recent work includes the new Museum of Marine Biology/Aquarium in Taiwan, and the Wuksachi Village at Sequoia, Kings Canyon National Park, California.

Foster and Partners
Riverside Three, 22 Hester Road, London, SW11 4AN, UK

Sir Norman Foster was born in Manchester, England, in 1935 and studied architecture and city planning at the University of Manchester and at Yale University. He established Team 4 in 1963 –

with his late wife, Wendy, and Su and Richard Rogers – and founded Foster Associates in 1967. Today he is internationally famous for his high-tech designs, many of which, such as the Hongkong and Shanghai Bank (1979–86), and Stansted Airport (1981–9) have resulted directly from competitions. Projects include the Sackler Galleries at the Royal Academy of Arts, London, which was named the RIBA building of the year in 1993; the Centre d'Art/Cultural Centre, Nîmes; the ITN Headquarters, London; Cranfield University Library; the new wing of the Joslyn Art Museum in Omaha, Nebraska, and the Cambridge University Law Faculty. Master plans include the King's Cross development and recently completed projects number the Reichstag remodelling, Berlin, and an airport at Chek Lap Kok for Hong Kong (covering an area of 1,248 hectares, this is the largest architectural scheme in the world). He is currently working on the Great Court of the British Museum and a Millennium Bridge in London. Norman Foster received a knighthood in the Queen's Birthday Honours in 1990, and his work has won over 60 awards and citations. In 1999 he became the 21st Pritzker Architecture Prize Laureate. He is a well-known figure on the international lecturing circuit. Although primarily concerned with large-scale architectural projects, Sir Norman Foster is also involved in furniture design.

gmp (von Gerkan, Marg & Partner)
139 Elbchausee, Hamburg, Germany

von Gerkan, Marg & Partner is one of the most successful architectural firms in Germany. Founder Meinhard von Gerkan was born in 1935 and studied in Berlin and Brunswick. In 1965 he began a collaboration with architect Volkwin Marg, and within the first year the team won seven first prizes in competitions, including one for the Berlin Tegel airport. The firm has been known as von Gerkan, Marg & Partner since 1972, and it has won over 90 national and international competitions and received numerous awards. GMP became internationally known as a team of airport architects but has designed small-scale homes, the interior of the Metropolitan Express Train, hotels, theatres and concert halls, office buildings and commercial centres, hospitals and research facilities, jumbo hangars and car parks, EXPO 2000 and the Fair grounds in Leipzig. The practice is also well-known for its masterplanning schemes such as those for Munich 21, Stuttgart 21 and Frankfurt 21. Meinhard von Gerkan has been the Professor at the Technical University of Brunswick since 1974. He is an Honorary Fellow of the American Institute of Architects and has been honoured by the Mexican Architectural Society.

GMW Partnership
PO Box 1613, 239 Kensington High Street, London W8 6SL, UK

GMW was founded as Gollins Melvin and Ward in 1949 and has 50 years experience in the design and procurement of new construction, refurbishment and fitting out of most building types in the UK and abroad. The group has experience in interior design, space-planning, furniture and product design. Clients include British American Tobacco, NatWest Bank, Citibank, First Choice Holidays, Reuters, CrestCo, Gerling Insurance and BAA. It has been honoured with various awards, most recently the British Council for Offices National Fitout Award for the BAT Headquarters.

Nicholas Grimshaw and Partners Ltd
1 Conway Street, Fitzroy Square, London W1P 6LR, UK

Nicholas Grimshaw founded his own practice in 1980, having already won acclaim for his industrial architecture with buildings for Citroen, Zanussi, Herman Miller and BMW. Today the firm handles a wider range of projects, including sports and leisure complexes, commercial and retail buildings and schemes in the fields of television and radio. Notable buildings include the Oxford Ice Rink, the Financial Times Printing Works, a new research facility for Xerox Research, the Combined Operations Centre for British Airways at Heathrow, the RAC Regional Headquarters in Bristol and the International Passenger Terminal for the Channel Tunnel trains at Waterloo Station. In 1982 the practice won the Sports Council's national competition for the design of standardized sports halls throughout the UK. Recently the practice has completed the Ludwig Erhard Haus (Berlin Stock Exchange and Communications Centre); the redevelopment of the existing Grandstand for Lord's Cricket Ground, the redevelopment of Manchester Airport's Terminal 1 and Heathrow's Terminal 3, offices and customer services centre for Hutchinson Telecom in Darlington and an office building for MABEG in Germany. Currently Grimshaw is working on many schemes amongst which is the masterplanning and redevelopment of Paddington Station, London, the redevelopment of Zurich Airport and a touring industrial design exhibition called FUSION as well as various Millennium Commission-funded projects. Nicholas Grimshaw and Partners has received many awards and commendations including a number from the Civic Trust, the Department of the Environment, the Royal Institute of British Architects and the Royal Fine Art Commission.

Hardy Holzman Pfeiffer Associates
902 Broadway, 19th Floor, New York, NY 10010, USA

HHPA was founded in 1967 by Hugh Hardy, Malcolm Holzman and Norman Pfeiffer. They have long been nationally recognized for their innovative designs of public spaces such as libraries, educational facilities, museums, theatres, concert halls and restaurants. They received early acclaim as leaders in the development of a new, distinctly American architecture being awarded the Arnold W. Brunner Prize in Architecture by the National Institute of Arts and Letters. Four years later they were given the Medal of Honor from the New York chapter of the American Institute of Architects, followed in 1981 by the AIA's prestigious Firm Honor Award. Since then they have been frequent recipients of major national prizes and have completed numerous major projects throughout the United States.

Steven Holl
435 Hudson Street, 4th Floor, New York, NY 10014, USA

Steven Holl was born in Bremerton, Washington, in 1947. He established Steven Holl Architects in New York in 1976. He is an honours graduate of the University of Washington. He studied architecture in Rome in 1970 and did post-graduate work at the Architectural Association in London in 1976. His work has formed the subject of major retrospectives in various museums within the United States, and the Museum of Modern Art in New York has purchased his drawings to add to their permanent collection. Holl has been the recipient of the National AIA Interiors Award for the offices of D. E. Shaw & Co. in New York and the National AIA Honor Award for Excellence in Design for the Texas Stretto House in Dallas. In 1993, Steven Holl Architects completed the winning design among 516 entries in the competition for the new Museum of Contemporary Art, Helsinki. Among his most recent prizes are the 1996 Progressive Architecture Award for Excellence in Design for the Knut Hamsun Museum in Bødo, Norway and for the Museum of the City in Cassina, Italy. Holl's Chapel of St Ignatius in Seattle, Washington, has been awarded the 1998 National AIA award for Design Excellence. Holl teaches at the Columbia University Graduate School of Architecture, at the University of Washington in Seattle and the Pratt Institute, New York.

Jestico + Whiles Architects
1 Cobourg Street, London NW1 2HP, UK

The architectural practice of Jestico + Whiles was founded in 1977 by principals Tom Jestico, John Whiles, Robert Collingwood and Tony Ingram and today has offices in London, Glasgow, Prague and Munich. Preoccupation with lightweight structures and components can be seen in early industrial projects at Epsom (1979) and Waltham Cross (1982), while later schemes for Friends of the Earth, the Policy Studies Institute and research for the UK Department of Energy represent the development of Jestico + Whiles' approach to the concept of low-energy workspaces. Further projects include a science and technology park in Scotland and several inner-city industrial/office buildings, including Gallery Court, Stukely Street and Jockey's Fields. Recent work numbers embassies and ambassador's residences in Latvia and Bulgaria; a major CrossRail station interchange, One Aldwych hotel in central London and their largest project to date – Burrell's Wharf, a £28-million residential and leisure development on a Grade II-listed site in London's docklands.

Joppien Dietz Architekten
Schaumainkai 69, D-60596 Frankfurt-am-Main, Germany

The architectural firm, Joppien Dietz was founded in 1989 by Albert Dietz, Anett Eisen-Joppien and Jörg Joppien, and the Berlin office was opened in 1992 in order to work on the Max-Schmeling-Halle. The current partnership of Dietz Joppien was set up by Albert Dietz and Anett Eisen-Joppien in 1997, when Jörg Joppien started Jörg Joppien Architekten. Dietz was born in 1958 in Saarbruken. He studied architecture at the Technischen Hochschule in Darmstadt and as a Fulbright Scholar received a Masters degree in Architecture from the University of Oregon. Anett Eisen-Joppien was born in 1959 in Frankfurt and studied at the Technischen Universitat in Berlin and the at the Hochschule in Darmstadt. She was also a Fulbright Scholar and received her Masters from the University of California at Berkeley. The practice specializes in residential, leisure and retail spaces as well as stations and airport buildings. Selected projects include a training centre in Rhein-Main airport, Frankfurt, an EXPO railway station in Hanover, the Finnish Pavilion at Expo 2000 and a station in Wolfsburg.

Kanner Architects
10924 Le Conte Avenue, Los Angeles, CA 90024, USA

Kanner Architects is a third-generation architectural practice located in Los Angeles. Kanner's projects range from retail interiors and shopping centres to restaurants and retail spaces, as well as office interiors and residential architecture and design. The practice was founded in 1946 by Hermann Kanner who died in 1953. His son Charles Kanner then led the firm until his death in 1998 and now Stephen Kanner is principal-in-charge. In 1998 a monograph, *Pop Architecture: Kanner Architects*, was published by Images Publishing Group.

Kauffmann Theilig & Partner
Zeppelinstrasse 10, Ostildern 73760, Stuttgart, Germany

Dieter Kauffmann was born in 1954 in Sindelfingen. After graduating from the Fachhochschule of Augsburg in 1978, he worked for architects in Stuttgart before taking up an appointment with Behnisch and Partner in 1980 where he remained until he joined Heinle, Wischer and Partner. In 1988, he went into partnership with Andreas Theilig. Theilig was born in Stuttgart in 1951. After graduating from the Technische Hochschule in Darmstadt in 1978 he worked briefly for architects in Darmstadt before also joining Behnisch and Partner. He has lectured at the Fachhochschule in Biberach.

Kiessler + Partner Architekten
Mauerkircherstrasse 41, 81679 Munich, Germany

Kiessler + Partner Architekten was founded in 1962 in Munich by Uwe Kiessler and Hermann Schultz. Kiessler was born in Krefeld and studied at the Technical University of Munich. He is a member of the Kuratorium Landschaftsschutz and of the Academy of Fine Arts in Berlin. Until 1990 Kiessler was a professor at the Fachhochschule in Munich and is currently professor of design and construction at the Technical University of Munich. Before entering into partnership Schultz also studied architecture at the Technical University of Munich. The practice is at present working on two museums – the Kunstsammlung Standehaus in Dusseldorf and the Umbau Villa Stuck in Munich.

Kiss + Zwigard Architects
60 Warren Street, Third Floor, New York, NY 10007, USA

Kiss + Zwigard Architects is involved in a wide range of projects from the interior design of single rooms to urban-scale developments. The practice was founded almost 20 years ago by Laszlo Kiss and Todd Zwigard who both trained at Cornell University and who now teach at Parsons School of Design in New York and at Columbia University. Kiss + Zwigard has designed numerous residential projects ranging from a 33rd-storey condominium in Manhattan to a Town Plan for Gibelina, Italy. The architects are specialists in loft design and have recently produced two loft conversions in the Tribeca neighbourhood of New York and a 12,000-square-foot private residence on the Upper

East Side. Their work has been honoured with numerous awards, among them two Progressive Architecture Awards for Excellence in Design in 1983 and 1984 and two American Institute of Architects Honor Awards from the New York chapter.

Eric R. Kuhne & Associates
York House, 23 Kingsway, London WC2B 6UJ, UK

Eric R. Kuhne & Associates is an international design consultancy which believes in the marriage of architecture, landscape and civic arts. Eric Kuhne is an architect, industrial designer, graphic designer, essayist and lecturer. He holds a BA in art and architecture from Rice University and a Masters of architecture from Princeton University. Recent projects include a riverfront development in Fort Wayne, Indiana, a residence on Chesapeake Bay, an office and entertainment complex in Sydney, Australia, and a major shopping complex in Kent, UK.

Kisho Kurokawa Architect & Associates
11F Aoyama Bldg, 1–2–3 Kita Aoyama, Minato-ku, Tokyo 107, Japan

Kisho Kurokawa was born in Nagoya in 1934 and studied architecture at Kyoto University. In 1960, while studying for a doctorate at Tokyo University, he formed the Metabolist Group, whose philosophy – closely linked with Buddhism – considered urban architectural forms as organisms capable of growth and change, a belief which is echoed in his designs to date, most notably: the National Bunraku Theatre, Osaka; the Roppongi Prince Hotel, Tokyo; the Japanese-German Culture Centre in Berlin and the National Museums of Modern Art in Nagoya, Hiroshima and Wakayama. As well as his architectural works, he has designed distinctive furniture for Tendo and Kosuga and created notable urban spaces such as the Silk Road Town of Nara Station and the Amagasaki Eco-Town in Hyogo. His works have been exhibited in New York, Paris, London, Dublin, Moscow, Milan, Florence, Rome, Budapest and Sofia and, most recently, at the Sackler Galleries at the Royal Academy of Arts in London. Kurokawa has just completed the Kuala Lumpur International Airport in Malaysia and a New Wing for the Van Gogh Museum, Amsterdam. He is a member of the Japan Institute of Architects and an Honorary Fellow of both the American Institute of Architects and the Royal Institute of British Architects and has received the Japan Literary Grand Prize and citations of excellence from the AIA for his 'Philosophy of Symbiosis' in 1992. He was decorated with the Order of Cultural Merit from the Government of Tokyo in 1999 as well as being made Honorary Professor of the South East University in China. He is a Chevalier de l'Ordre des Arts et des Lettres and in 1997 was given the World Best Architecture Award by the FIABCI.

Daniel Libeskind
Windscheidstrasse 18, D-10627, Berlin, Germany

Daniel Libeskind was born in Poland in 1946 and became an American citizen in 1965. He studied music in Israel and in New York where he became a virtuoso performer. He went on to study architecture at the Cooper Union and received a postgraduate degree in the history and theory of architecture from the School of Comparative Studies at Essex

University in 1972. Libeskind founded his practice in Berlin in 1990 since which time he has been involved in urban, architectural and cultural projects. He has taught and lectured at many universities worldwide and is currently professor at the Hochschule für Gestaltung, Karlsruhe, as well as the Louis Kahn Professor at Yale University. In 1986 Libeskind founded and directed the Architecture Intermunidium, a private, non-profit institute for architectural urbanism in Milan. He was appointed a senior scholar to the John Paul Getty Centre and is a member of the Akademie der Kunst and the European Academy of Arts and Letters. Recent schemes include the Jewish Museum in Berlin, a museum in Osnabrueck and the Felix Nussbaum Haus. He is currently working on the Spiral Extension to the Victoria and Albert Museum in London, the Imperial War Museum North in Manchester, the Bremen Philharmonic Hall, the Jewish Museum in San Francisco and the JVC University Schools of Public Policy, Teacher Training and Architecture in Guadalajara, Mexico. Libeskind has been the recipient of numerous awards, most recently the 1999 Deutsche Architekturpreis for the Jewish Museum in Berlin.

Peter Lorenz
Maria Theresien Strasse 37, Innsbruck, A-6020 Austria

Peter Lorenz was born in Innsbruck in 1950 and received a Masters degree in architecture from the University of Venice. He has had his own practice since 1980 and today has offices in Innsbruck and Vienna. He has completed over 200 projects ranging from housing schemes to retail outlets and offices and has recently undertaken city planning and large urban schemes. He is a lecturer at various universities and frequently holds workshops and study trips worldwide.

MacCormac Jamieson Prichard
9 Heneage Street, Spitalfields, London E1 5LJ, UK

MacCormac Jamieson Prichard was founded in 1972 by Richard MacCormac (born 1938), Peter Jamieson (born 1939) and David Prichard (born 1948). Both MacCormac and Jamieson studied at Cambridge University and at University College, London, and Prichard trained at the Bartlett School of Architecture, London, where he is now RIBA external examiner. MacCormac was president of the Royal Institute of British Architects until 1993 and has taught and lectured widely. Jamieson teaches at Cambridge University. The practice encompasses a broad range of building types, from highly crafted buildings for Oxford and Cambridge colleges to offices, public buildings, housing for both the public and private sectors and large commercial projects, such as the redevelopment of Spitalfields Market in London. MJP has prepared master plans and urban designs for sites such as Paternoster Square and King's Cross in London, for green field sites in new towns and for reclaimed land in London's docklands. The practice has published a number of articles on architecture, urban regeneration and planning and in particular on the relationship of new architecture to historic settings. It has also carried out research into office design, energy efficiency and land use. Recent projects include the Cable and Wireless Training College in Coventry, the Ruskin Library in Lancaster, the Wellcome Wing for the Science Museum in London, buildings for Oxford and Cambridge colleges, and the Jubilee Line station which will serve the new London Bankside Tate Gallery.

Mahmoudieh Design
Kurfürstendamm 37, 10719 Berlin, Germany

Yasmine Mahmoudieh was born in Germany. She studied art history in Florence, architecture at the Ecole d'Intérieur in Geneva, interior design at the College of Nôtre Dame in Belmont, as well as architecture and interior design at the University of California in Los Angeles where she received her diploma. She co-founded the Architectural Design Group International in 1986 and the following year she founded her own company based in Los Angeles. Today Mahmoudieh Design has offices in Hamburg, Berlin and Barcelona and is due to open a branch in London. The practice designs restaurants, exhibition and fair stands, houses and furniture. It also undertakes the interior design of hotels and office buildings. Selected projects include the Kempinski Hotel, Bad Saarow, Germany; the Millennium Centre in Budapest, Hungary; offices for Garbe KG in Hamburg, Germany; 'The Factory' in Berlin (conversion of an old mill into galleries, restaurants, offices and lofts), and the Gordon Eckhard Production Studios in Hollywood, California. Recently Mahmoudieh undertook the renovation of the SAS Radisson Hotel in Copenhagen and also worked on the interior design of a new hotel for people with disabilities located on the outskirts of Berlin, as well as a shopping centre outside London.

Pierluigi Piu
Via E. Besta 6, Cagliari 09129, Italy

Pierluigi Piu graduated from the architectural department of Florence University. He worked as a freelance architect until becoming a partner in Atelier Proconsolo in 1982. In 1985 he worked as Associate Consultant for ACME Consultants since which time he has also collaborated with Art & Build in Brussels and with Steven Beckers, also in Belgium. His work is mainly with small-scale retail and domestic spaces as well as on product design.

Antoine Predock Architect
300 Twelfth Street, NW, Albuquerque, New Mexico, 87102, USA

Antoine Predock studied at the University of New Mexico, Albuquerque, and at Columbia University, New York, and founded his own practice in 1967. He is a Fellow of the American Institute of Architects and his work has received numerous awards and citations. Projects include the Institute of American Indian Arts, Santa Fe, New Mexico; the Student Affairs and Administrative Services Building at the University of California, Santa Barbara; the New Mexico Hispanic Cultural Centre in Albuquerque; the Civic Arts Plaza in the City of Thousand Oaks, California, and the Spencer Theater in Ruidoso, New Mexico. He has held educational positions at various universities in the United States, including Harvard and UCLA. Predock is also a registered landscape architect and interior designer. In 1989 he opened a second office in Venice, California. Predock's work has been published and has exhibited widely.

Sander Architecten
Herengracht 66, 1015 BR Amsterdam, The Netherlands

Ellen Sander studied architecture at the Technical University in Delft. She worked for Urban Development Service and Benthem Crouwel Architects in Amsterdam before establishing Sander Architecten in 1990. Recent projects include housing in Leidschenveen, the interior conversion of a surgical out-patients' clinic of the University Hospital in Groningen, a new farm development at Holysloot and the expansion/adaption of Media Plaza 2000 in the Trade Fair Building in Utrecht.

Schwartz Architects
180 Varick Street, New York, NY 10014, USA

Frederic Schwartz received his Masters degree in architecture from Harvard University and is a graduate of the University of California at Berkeley. His practice has been selected by both *Architectural Digest* and *Metropolitan Home* magazines as one of the top 100 design firms. Schwartz is the recipient of the Rome Prize in Architecture and the '40 under 40' award. He has exhibited his work in both the Venice and Paris Biennales. Recent projects include the headquarters for the ad agency Deutsch Inc. in New York, the Go Overboard shop at the Shedd Aquarium, Chicago, in collaboration with EHDD, and a masterplan, buildings and park for the recently completed Capitol of Southwest France in Toulouse. Schwartz Architects is currently working on the Staten Island Ferry Terminal in New York.

Claudio Silvestrin Limited
392 St John Street, London EC1V 4NN, UK

Claudio Silvestrin was born in 1954 and trained in Milan at AG Fronzoni. He completed his studies at the Architectural Association in London where he now lives and works. He teaches at the Bartlett School of Architecture in London and at the Ecole Supérieure d'Art Visuels in Lausanne. He has realized projects worldwide and some of his most important works include shops for Giorgio Armani (Paris), offices, shops and a home for Calvin Klein (Paris, Milan and New York) and projects for museums and art galleries.

Stanton Williams
Diespeker Wharf, 38 Graham Street, London N1 8JX, UK

Stanton Williams has a strong reputation for work on notable and prestigious projects, and for the high quality of its design work and creative use of space, light and materials. Recent projects include the award-winning headquarters building for Leo Burnet Advertising in London (recipient of the British Council for Offices 1997 'Office of the Year' Award) and the Millennium Commission's Landmark Seed Bank project currently under construction at the Royal Botanic Gardens in Sussex. The company was founded by Alan Stanton and Paul Williams in 1966. Stanton studied at the Architectural Association in London and at the University of California. He worked with Richard Rogers and Renzo Piano on the Pompidou Centre from 1970 to 1977, and in collaboration with Mike Down designed an exhibition space in the Museum of Science and Industry at La Villette in Paris. Before this he worked for Foster Associates and as Partner in the architectural firm Chrysalis in Los Angeles. Paul Williams studied at Birmingham College of Art and later at the Yale Arts Centre. He worked as head of design at the Victoria and Albert Museum in London and in private practice, where he was involved primarily in the design of exhibition spaces and installations, including shows at the Hayward Gallery, the Royal Academy of Arts, the refurbishment of the Introductory Galleries at Luton Hoo and the Japanese Primary Gallery at the Victoria and Albert Museum.

Studio MG Architects
101 Turnmill Street, Fourth Floor, London EC1M 5QP, UK

Studio MG Architects was established as a practice in 1995 by John Grimes and Craig Moffat. The practice has projects that range from small residential commissions to high-budget commercial projects. Recent schemes include adding a glass atrium, a cinema, shops and galleries to the new Guildenburgh Leisure Centre in Peterborough, UK. It is currently working on a new restaurant for Wiseguys Ltd. as an extension to its already successful bar, Home, in London. Grimes and Moffat both taught at the Mackintosh School of Architecture, Glasgow, and at Oxford Brookes University.

STUDIOS Architecture
99 Green Street, San Francisco, California 94111 USA

STUDIOS Architecture was founded in 1985 by Darryl T. Roberson, Erik Sueberkrop, Gene Rae and Phillip Olson and today has offices in San Francisco, Washington, New York, London and Paris. Recent projects include the Milpitas City Hall in Silicon Valley, a one million-square-foot office campus development in San Francisco and interiors for the new Shanghai Grand Theatre. STUDIOS also designs corporate interiors for many prominent law firms, financial concerns and high-tech companies in the USA, Europe and Asia, including Apple Computers, Silicon Graphics, Arnold & Porter, Morgan Stanley & Company, American Express, 3Com Corporation, Andersen Consulting and Nike. The practice has received numerous American Institute of Architects Merit Awards, and its work has been published in leading design magazines in Europe and the USA.

Shin Takamatsu Architect and Associates
36–4 Jyobadaiin-cho, Takeda, Fushimi-ku, Kyoto 612, Japan

Shin Takamatsu was born in 1948 in Shimane Prefecture, Japan. He trained at Kyoto University and in 1977 established the Takumi Design Office. He has held educational positions at Fukui Technical University, Osaka College of Art's architectural department and was Assistant Professor of the Kyoto Seika University until 1991. Shin Takamatsu Architect and Associates was founded in 1980, the Takamatsu Planning Office in 1988 and Takamatsu & Layani Architects Associates in Berlin in 1992. Takamatsu's work has received considerable acclaim both within Japan (he was given the Kyoto Prefecture Meritorious Cultural Service Award in 1994 and the Education Minister's Art Encouragement Prize in 1996) and internationally. Takamatsu became an Honorary Fellow of the American Institute of Architects in 1995 and of the Bund Deutscher Architeckten in 1997. The same year he obtained a PhD in engineering from Kyoto University and was made Professor of Kyoto University, School of Architecture. He has exhibited in Europe and the

United States, having had solo shows at the San Francisco Museum of Modern Art and the Aedes Gallery in Germany.

Rafael Viñoly Architects

50 Vandam Street, New York, NY 10013, USA

Rafael Viñoly was born in Montevideo, Uruguay, He studied architecture at the University of Buenos Aires and founded his own practice, Estudio de Arquitectura, with six associates. It quickly became one of the largest architectural firms in South America and by 1974 Viñoly had won over 50 competitions. He studied for a Masters degree and taught at the University of Buenos Aires until the military coup of 1974 when he left and organized an alternative architecture school. Viñoly went to the United States four years later as a guest lecturer at Washington University and then at the Harvard Graduate School of Design. He created his own firm the following year. His work ranges from private residences and retail interiors to university buildings, courthouses, a performing arts centre and corporate headquarters. His largest project to date is the Tokyo International Forum, which was completed in 1996. Recent schemes include a sports stadium for Princeton University, a mixed-use office building in Beijing and the re-zoning of a 1.6 million square-foot development in Manhattan. He has received numerous awards, most recently the 1995 Medal of Honor and the 1996 Excellence in Design awards from the AIA.

Virgile & Stone Associates Ltd

25 Store Street, South Crescent, London
WC1E 7BL, UK

Virgile & Stone Associates Ltd is an international design consultancy specializing in retail, restaurant, hotel, showroom, leisure and workplace environments. The firm was founded in 1980 by Carlos Virgile and Nigel Stone since which time it has built up an impressive client base that includes Hugo Boss, Wedgwood, Groupe Chez Gérard and the De Bijenkorf chain of stores in The Netherlands. Recent schemes include new department stores in Germany for Breuninger and for De Bijenkorf in Amstelveen; a new concept for Chez Gérard restaurants; retail projects for Heal's, London; a restaurant and bar for restaurateur Stephen Bull and an exhibition showcase for world-renowned watchmaker Patek Philippe for the Basel Fair in Switzerland. It is currently undertaking the main restaurant of the Oberoi Towers Hotel in Mumbai, India as well as an extensive graphics projects for a themed restaurant within the same hotel. Its innovative retail concept for Schipol Airport's Central Lounge opened in September 1999. Together with Benthem Crouwel (the airport's Dutch architects) Virgile & Stone Associates is now involved on the development of a new shopping centre in Amsterdam, the Villa Arena. In addition it has been commissioned by Andersen Consulting to work alongside the architect Sir Norman Foster and space-planners Studios on the interiors of its new headquarters.

Clive Wilkinson Architects

101 South Robertson Blvd, Ste 204, Los Angeles, California 90048, USA

Clive Wilkinson founded his own practice in Los Angeles in 1991. Previously he had worked with Frank Gehry as joint project manager on the Walt Disney Concert Hall. He specializes in creative office space, entertainment facilities, television stations and high-tech office development projects. His design for TBWA/Chiat/Day offices on the US West Coast received much acclaim internationally and has been followed by various commissions including redevelopment work for Twentieth Century Fox studios, a small office building for a film production company in Venice, new offices for an advertising agency in Ludwigsburg, Germany, and the worldwide headquarters of the advertising giant Ogilvy & Mather. In 1999 Clive Wilkinson opened an office in New York under the management of senior associate Ali Hocek and undertook the extensive remodelling of the TBWA/Chiat/Day offices in New York. Since 1991 the practice has completed various urban design schemes such as those for Elstree Studios in London and an award-winning proposal for the Perth Waterfront in Australia.

Alberto Aspesi showroom
Milan, Italy

Architect: Antonio Citterio and Partners

Project team: Antonio Citterio, Patricia Viel. Client: Alberto Aspesi SpA. General contractor: Estedil srl. Lighting consultant: Studio Light. Lighting: Staff; I Guzzini. Lighting fixtures: Flos. Steel hanging structures: Marzoratti & Ronchetti. Tables: B&B Italia. Chairs: Zanotta. Installation: *Coccodrillo* by Mario Merz. Silkscreen: *Mao Tse Tung* by Andy Warhol. Additional artworks: Mimmo Rotella, Mario Schifano.

Alexandre Hercovitch shop
São Paulo, Brazil

Architect: Studio Arthur de Mattos Casas

Collaborating Designer: Silvia Carmesini. Client: Alexandre Hercovitch. Main contractor: Lock (engineering). Polyurethane floors: Resin Floor. Lighting design: Opera Prima. MDF panels: Duratex

Brooklyn Academy of Music Rose Cinemas
Brooklyn, New York, USA

Architect: Hardy Holzman Pfeiffer Associates

Project team: Hugh Hardy (partner-in-charge), Pamela Loeffelman (project manager), Steve Maisano (project architect), Kris Nikolich, Jason Chang (design team), Caroline Bertrand (interiors). Client: Brooklyn Academy of Music. Construction manager: Lehrer McGovern Bovis. Structural engineer: Robert Silman Associates. MEP engineer: Altieri Sebor Wieber Consulting Engineers. Graphic design: Pentagram. Theatre consultant: Boston Light and Sound Inc. Ausio-visual consultant: Cerami Associates. Lighting design: Cline Bettridge Bernstein Lighting Design Inc. Café chairs and tables: L&B. Café lighting: CBB. Café rug: David Shaw Nicholas. Club chairs: Cabot Wren. Floor lamp: Donghia. Graphics: Sign Designers of New York. Kiosk: Zero. Lamp: C. Bertrand Inc. Lighting: Rejuvenation Lamp and Fixture Co. Nets: Archs Lightmakers. Cinema seats: Country Roads. Side and coffee tables: Brayton. Sofa: Cabor Wren. Theatre carpet: Masland Contract. Upholstery: Kravet.

barnesandnoble.com
New York City, USA

Architect: Anderson Architects

Project team: Ross Anderson (principal), M. J. Sagan (associate), Todd Stodolski (project architect), Matthew Greer, Caroline Otto, Peony Quan, Andrew Benner, Abigail Banker, Jon Maass, Shane Braddock, Paul Henderson. Client: Barnes and Noble Inc. Construction manager: Lehr Construction. Interiors consultant: D. L. Design. Structural engineer: Gilsanz Murray Steficek. Mechanical engineer: Jack Green Associates. Acoustic/technology consultant: Shen Milsom & Wilke Inc. Lighting consultant: Kugler Tillotson Associates. System furniture: Unifor. Inc. Custom furniture: Jonas Milder. Metal deck: Wildeck. Ceramic tile: Mannington. Carpets: Atlas. Blackboard: New York Blackboard. Window Shades: Sol-R-Shade. Lighting: Zumtobel-Staff; Delray; Lightolier; Hubbell, Legion Lighting, Exterior Vert; Rambusch; National.

Bene Showroom
London, UK

Architects: Apicella Associates (now Pentagram)

Project team: Lorenzo Apicella, Hilary Clark, Matthew Foster. Client: Bene Office Furniture. Main contractor: Shannon and Co Shopfitters. Structural engineer: Alan Conisbee & Associates. M&E engineer: Fulcrum Consulting. Lighting consultant and fittings: Zumtobel Staff Lighting; Interface Europe (floor); Burgess Architectural Products (ceiling).Staircase: Sovereign Stainless Fabrications.

Bluewater shopping centre
London, UK

Architect: Eric R. Kuhne Associates

Project architect: Benoy Architects. Client: Lend Lease. Associates architects: Brettell Jackson & Associates (HoF); Brooker Flynn Architects (JLP); GHM Rock Townsend (multiplex); Leach Rhodes Walker (C&A); RTKL (M&S); Design Solution (mall finishes concept); Fitch (Waterstone's); BDG McColl (South Village). Main contractor: Bluewater Construction Management Team. Environmental consultant: Battle McCarthy. Quantity surveyor: Cyril Sweett & Partners. Consulting engineers: Halcrow. Acoustics: Sandy Brown Associates. Lighting: Speirs & Major. Landscape: Townshend. Civil/structural engineer: Waterman Partnership. Roof/glazing: EAG; Prater Roofing. Roof membrane: Sarnafil. Aluminium roof: Hoogovens. Atrium glazing: Sky Systems; Space Decks. Glazing/curtain wall: Dane Architectural; Stewart Frazier. Doors/ironmongery: Hillson. Limestone floors: Steinindustrie Vetter. Balustrading: Alan Dawson Associates; Barker Shepley; Tecscreen. Ceilings: Riverside Mouldings; Clarke & Fenn; Jonathan James; Thermofelt. Metalwork: Gravesham Engineering. Faux stone painting: Lucas. Joinery: Abacus; Henry Venables. Metalwork: Littlehampton Welding; A.R. Dibley. Lighting: Zumtobel Staff; Enliten; We-Es; Oldham; Philips; Wila.

Bright Child
Santa Monica, California, USA

Architects: Kanner Architects

Project team: Stephen H. Kanner, Verr Bateman-Soltes. Associate architect: Michael Kovac Architect. Client: Bright Child. General contractor: Roger Ward Construction. Structural engineer: J. S. Chung. Playstructure: Prime Play.

British American Tobacco Headquarters
London, UK

Architects: GMW Partnership (Gollins Melvin Ward)

Project team: Lyn Edwards, John Bevan, David Hughes, Ron Russell, Timothy Hardingham, Susy Phillips. Client: British American Tobacco. Building owner: Hammerson UK Properties. Cost consultant: Davis Langdon & Everest. Services engineer: Hoare Lea & Partners. Furniture: Ergonom Dialogue (cellular offices); Ahrend Ltd. (open-plan areas); Coexistence (loose furniture). Partitions: Faram Ltd. Carpet: Westbond.

Broadgate Club West
London, UK

Architect: Allford Hall Monaghan Morris Architecture

Project team: Simon Allford, Reenie Elliot, Jonathan Hall, Viktor Kite, Viktor Johanssen, Susan LeGood, Paul Monaghan, Peter Morris, Louise Munch, Steve Perkins, Nina Quesnel. Client: The Broadgate Club plc.; The British Land Company. Main contractor: Kvaerner Trollope and Colls. Quantity surveyor: Davis Langdon & Everest. Services engineer: Monal Associates. Structural engineer: CCP Consulting Engineers. Acoustic consultant: Arup Acoustics. Graphic design: Studio Myerscough. Furniture design: Stafford. Torch design: Eleanor Kearney. Services: Inner City Environmental. External cladding and blue wall glazing: Pollards Fyrespan. Blue wall lighting and audio-visual equipment: Atmospherics. Stone flooring, wall and floor ceramic tiling: Marriott & Price. Gym equipment: Life Fitness. Ironmongery: Allgoods. Metal panel ceilings: Durlum. Furniture: Conran Contracts. Joinery: Trollope & Colls Elliot. Specialist joinery: Charles Barrett Interiors. Lockers, saunas and steam rooms: Dalesauna. Timber floors: Tarkett. Specialist metalwork: Qualart.

Calyx & Corolla Headquarters
San Francisco, USA

Architect: STUDIOS Architecture

Project team: Cathy Barrett, Gail Napell, Russell Zeidner, Heidi Peterson, Angela Blosen. Client: Calyx & Corolla. Associate architect: Hannum & Associates. Main contractor: Swinerton and Walberg. Engineering team: Paganini Electric Corporation; Acco. Floral carpet: Prince Street. Executive office carpet: Bentley. Furniture: Knoll. Breakroom pendant lighting: Delray Lighting. Corridor sconces at call centre: Stonco. Breakroom flooring: Armstrong. Breakroom seating ICF. Call centre uplighting: Wellmade. Executive floor sconces: Terzani.

Cinema Atelier am Bollwerk
Stuttgart, Germany

Architect: Behnisch, Sabatke, Behnisch

Project team: Professor Günter Behnisch, Stefan Behnisch, Günther Schaller Client: Kinoverwaltung Erasmus. Collaborating architect: Büro Ohlf (site supervision). Contractors: Messrs. Kinoten (cinema technology); Messrs. Bader (dry construction); Schlosser Mayer (metalwork 1); Gaukler + Herdrich (metalwork 2); Messrs. Zeeb (carpenter); Fritz-Herre GmbH (wooden floors/cinema); Schon + Hippelein (natural stone). Structural engineers: Leonhardt; Andrä + Partner. Electrical engineers: Ing. Büro Schwarz. Environmental engineers: Rentschler Riedesser. Building physics:Büro Bobran.

Cleveland Public Library
Cleveland, Ohio, USA

Architect: Hardy Holzman Pfeiffer Associates.

Project team: Malcolm Holzman (partner-in-charge), Kala Somvanshi (project manager), Robert Almodovar (project manager and architect), Setrak Ohannessian (project architect), Daria Pizzetta, Robin Kunz (interiors), Allen Robinson, Victor Rodriguez, Manuel Mergal, Bruce Spenadel, Rob Lopez, Mike Connolly, Jeff Porten, Kristopher Nikolich, Christopher Bach (design team), Nancy Geng, Susan Pon (interiors team). Architect of record:

URS Griner. Historical architect: Robert P Madison International. Client: Cleveland Public Library. Civil engineering and construction administration: Ralph C. Tyler, Co. Lighting consultant: Fisher Marantz Renfro Stone. Landscape architect: Hanna Olin Ltd. Construction manager: Turner Construction Company. Curtain wall consultant: Heitmann & Associates. Acoustical consultant: Acentech. Architectural conservationist: Lou. A. Maranella & Associates. Graphic designer: Salestrom Design Inc. Carpet tiles in Stokes Wing: Shaw Carpet. Rugs in Main Building: Spinning Wheel Carpets. Solid flooring: Forbo Industries. Marble flooring: Georgia Marble. Interior glass: Bendheim. Custom reading tables, reading chairs and millwork: Agati, Inc. Lounge chairs: Rialto. Computer task chairs: Olivetti. Staff workstations: Steelcase. Auditorium seating: Country Roads. Carpet tiles in Main Building: Milliken Carpets.

de Barones Shopping Centre
Breda, The Netherlands

Architect: CZWG

Project team: Rex Wilkinson; Ray Stuart. Site architect: Kraaijvanger Urbis. Client: MAB Groep BV; Vroom and Dreesmann; Municipality of Breda. Main contractor: Heijmans Bouw. Construction manager: Kats & Waalwijk. Structural engineer: Grabowsky & Poort BV. Services engineer: Smits Van Burgst. Graphic design: Cuba Design. Lighting consultant: Lighting Design Partnership. Custom-made door furniture: Re:Form. Rooflights: Kalwall.

Empty Design Office
Madrid, Spain

Architect: Victor López Cotelo Arquitecto

Project team: Pedro Morales Falmouth, Isabel Mira Pueo. Client: Francisco Mínguez Coll, Empty SL. Construction firm: Empty SL. Structures: Mavi. Masonry: Frontera SL. Lighting and electricity: Instalaciones Merino. Air-conditioning: Danaire. Carpentry: La Navarra. Metalwork: Mavi. Artworks: Miguel Gonzalez. Finishing: Empty SL. Furniture: Luis Díaz Mauriño; Francisco Mínguez Coll., manufactured by La Navarra.

Gardermoen Airport
Oslo, Norway

Architect: Aviaplan – joint venture between Narud-Stokke-Wiig Arkitekter Planleggere; Niels Torp Arkitekter; Skaarup & Jespersen Arkitekter & Byplanlaeggere; Calvert & Clark Architects; Bjorbekk & Lindheim As, Landscape Architects; and Hjellnes Cowi.

Project team: Gudmund Stokke (project leader), Hans Haagensen, Niels Torp, Ole Wiig (concept group); John Arne Bjerknes (design co-ordinator); Ole Tørklep (project co-ordinator); Geoffrey Clark (Calvert and Clark Architects – technical co-ordinator); Bernhard Dahle/Torben S. Jensen (project administrator); John Arne Bjerknes (central building); Per Suul (Pier); Pal Laurantzon (railway station); Christian Henriksen (external skin); Jan Ellef Søyland (internal work); Ninni Gøranson (internal fittings); Roald Sand (logistics); Geoffrey Clark (baggage handling); Åke Letting (Astrup & Hellern – technical areas). Client: Oslo Lufthavn AS (OSL) – subsidiary of the Norwegian Civil Aviation Administration. Structural design: Ove Arup & Partners. Engineers: Reinertsengruppen. Lighting design: Lighting Design Partnership. Baggage

Handling: Paul Benefield, Greiner Eng.

Geffrye Museum Extension
London, UK

Architect: Branson Coates Architecture Ltd

Branson Coates (concept); Sheppard Robson (executive architects). Project team: Doug Branson, Nigel Coates, Gerrard O'Carroll, Simon Vernon-Harcourt, David Hughes, Christian Ducker, Allan Bell. Client: the Geffrye Museum. Main contractor: Kier London. Project manager: Davis Langdon Management. Quantity surveyors: Davis Langdon & Everest. Mechanical and electrical engineers: Max Fordham and Partners. Structural engineers: Alan Baxter and Associates. Exhibition designer: Ronayne Design. Graphic designer: Sally McIntosh. Contractor Phase 1: Duffy Construction.

Go Overboard shop
Chicago, USA

Architect: Schwartz Architects; Esherick Homsey Dodge & Davis (EHDD/Chicago)

Project team Schwartz Architects: Frederic Schwartz (principal -in-charge), Paul Cali (associate-in-charge), Leslie Ghym (senior project designer), Bruno Arnold, Shane Braddock, Steven Petrides; Maggie Mahboubian, Tamie Naponen (models). Project team Esherick Homsey Dodge & Davis: Charles M. Davis (principal-in-charge), Marc L'Italien (project designer/manager), Pierre Zetterberg (principal-in-charge), Kim Swanson, Amy Storek, Orla Huq, Glennis Briggs. Client: The John G.Shedd Aquarium. Main contractor: McClier Corporation. Subcontractors: Barsanti Woodwork Corp. (built-in and freestanding wood/glass merchandise display units); The Museum Professions Inc. (fiberglass octopus fabrication and installation); The Larson Co., (fiberglass sea creatures fabrication and installation). Structural engineers: Klein and Hoffmann Inc. MEP engineers: Environmental Systems Design Inc. Lighting consultants: Schuler & Shook Inc. Graphic design: Alexander Isley Inc. Costing: Oppenheim Lewis Inc.

HAL 9000 Cemex Computer Centre
Monterrey, Mexico

Architect: Nicholas Grimshaw & Partners Ltd

Project team: Nicholas Grimshaw, Ingrid Bille, Kai Flander, Angelika Kovacic, Eoin Billings. Client: Cemex. Site architects: Officina de Arquitectura. Structural engineer: Techniker. Quantity surveyor: Davis, Langdon & Everest. Lighting designer: Jonathan Speirs & Partner. Air-conditioning: Arco. Stainles-steel mesh cladding: GKD. Raised floor: Nesite. Textile ceiling: Kluth. Furniture: Unifor; Herman Miller. Sail wall: Lucas Sails. Special steel work: Wensum.

Hermès
Lille, France

Architect: Rena Dumas Architecture Intérieure.

Project team: Rena Dumas, Marleen Homan. Client: Hermès. Main contractor: BEMB Group. Lighting: Cosil. Mechanical engineering: C7 Bât. Structural engineering: SERC. Skylight structure: Marc Malinowsky. Cabinet-makers: Technic Agencement.

Interpolis
Tilburg, The Netherlands

Architect: Abe Bonnema, Bureau for Architecture and Environmental Planning BV

Project Team: Abe Bonnema. Interior designer: Kho Liang le Associates. Client: Interpolis. Main contractor: Bouwcominatie BBF – Heijmans Bouw V.O.F. Layout consultants: Veldhoen Facility Consultants BV. Landscape architects: West 8. Consultants: Deerns Consulting Engineers BV; Technisch Adviesbureau Becks (W & E technology); Adviesburo Peutz & Associes BV (building physics); Aronshon Consulting Engineers BV (construction), Prof Dr. W. H. Crouwel (art). Artists: Guido Geelen, Niek Kemps.

Issey Miyake Pleats Please
London, UK

Architect: Stanton Williams

Project team: Alan Farlie, Jane Houghton, Alan Stanton, Paul Williams. Client: Issey Miyake. Main contractor: Shinn and Setford. Structural engineer: Michael Chester Associates. Mechanical engineer: Michael Popper Associates. Quantity surveyor: Stockdale. Lighting design: Lightwaves. Flooring: Wallis Wood Floors. Metalwork: Marshall Howard; John Gill. Perspex drawer units: Thompson Plastics. Graphics: Service. Glass wall and shopfront: Shopfront Services. Stainless-steel floor panels: Ruddy Joinery. Joinery: Mid Sussex Joinery. Ironmongery: Allgood.

The Jewish Museum
Berlin, Germany

Architect: Daniel Libeskind

Project team: Matthias Reese, Jan Dinnebier (project manager); Stefan Blach, David Hunter, Tarla MacGabhann, Noel McCauley, Claudia Reisenberger, Eric J. Schall, Solveig Scheper, Ilkka Tarkkanen. Client: Berlin Senate of Culture. Main contractors: Fischer-Bau; Trube & Kings; Sponheuer GmbH. Landscape: Muller, Knippschild, Wehberg. Quantity surveyor: Alexander Lubic. Furniture: Daniel Libeskind.

Johan Restaurant
Graz, Austria

Architect: Claudio Silvestrin

Project team: Claudio Silvestrin, Mark Treharne, Douglas Tuck. Client: Johan GmbH. Builder/engineer: F. Robier. Table design: AG Fronzoni(1960s). Lighting: Claudio Silvestrin.

Kiasma Museum of Contemporary Art
Helsinki, Finland

Architect: Steven Holl Architects

Project team: Steven Holl, Vesa Honkonen (project architect), Tim Bade, Molly Blieden, Janet Cross, Tomoaki Tanaka, Stephen Cassell, Pablo Castro-Estévez, Lisina Fingerhuth, Mario Gooden, Tom Jenkinson, Jan Kinsbergen Justin Korhammer, Anderson Lee, Chris McVoy, Anna Müller, Kyong Paik, Justin Rüssli, Terry Surjan, Tapani Talo. Collaborating architect: Juhani Pallasmaa Ky. Project Team: Juhani Pallasmaa, Timo Kiukkola (project architect), Heikki

Määttanen, Seppo Mäntylä, Timo Ruusuvuori, Seppo Sivula. Main contractor: Seicon Oy. Electrical engineer: Tauno Nissinen Oy. Structural and mechanical consultant: Ove Arup & Partners Consulting Engineers. Lighting consultant: L'Observatorie International. Glass consultant: Engineering Office Aulis Bertin Ltd. Theatre technical consultant: Teatek. Acoustical consultant: Arkkitehtitoimisto Alpo Halme. Fixed furniture: U. J. Saarni Oy. Signage: Versaali Oy. Cast aluminium objects: Jarmo Saarekas. Glazing: Lounais-Hämeen Lasipalvelu Oy. Terrazzo floors: Suomen Maassalattiat Oy. Concrete floors: Lattiavirines Oy. Linoleum and plastic floor: RTV-Yhtymä Oy. Wood flooring: Parkettikeskus Oy. Stone work: Kivitimo Oy.

Kuala Lumpur International Airport.
Kuala Lumpur, Malaysia

Architects: Kisho Kurokawa; Akitek Jururancang

Project team: Kisho Kurokawa; Akitek Jururancang (Malaysia) Sdn. Bhd (concept architect and architectural design); Malaysian Japanese Airport Consortium (project architect); BDG McColl (collaborating architect responsible for interiors detailing, signage, fixed furniture of main terminal and contact pier). Client: Kuala Lumpur International Airport Berhad; PTKSH Contracting Consortium. Main Contractors: Taisei Corporation (Terminal Building and Contact Pier); Takenaka Corporation (Satellite). Mechanical engineering: Ranhill Bersekutu Sdn Bhd. Civil and reinforced concrete structural design: Sepakat Setia Perunding Sdn. Bhd. Landscape design: Arklandskap. Sign design: GK Sekkei; Lim Kok Wing Integrated. Main Terminal: Curtain wall: Fujisash and Shin Nikkei. Structural glazing: Central Glass and Aluminium. Granite flooring: Prime Granite. Ceramic tiling: Niro Ceramic. Satellite Building: Concrete structure: Ho Hup Construction. Steel structure: Tomoe Value. Cladding, skylight glazing, screens: YKK Industries. Public area metal strip ceiling: API. Granite floor: China Engineers. Metalwork: Angkasa Jasa. VIP lounge lighting consultant: Lighting Point.

Literaturhaus
Munich, Germany

Architect: Kiessler + Partner Architekten

Project Team: Uwe Kiessler, Hermann Schultz, Vera Ilic, Ursula Baptista, Markus Link. Client: Stiftung Buch-, Medien- und Literaturhaus. Contractors: Büro Steinberger, CBP (engineers); Haase + Söhmisch (landscape/open areas). Steelwork: Stahlbau Wolf GmbH. Archive System: Arbitec GmbH. Windows: Josef Bachhuber & Co. Column detailing: August Böhm. Sunblinds: Clauss Markisen. Stonemason: FGV Steinmetz und Bildhauer GmbH. Stone supply: Granitwerke Leonhard Jakob KG. Façade and façade restoration: Neumayr Stahl und Leicht Metallbau GmbH. Historical restoration: Fa Erwin Wiegerling. Café chairs: Model Czech by Thonet. Table and fitted furniture: Kiessler & Partner. Chairs on top floor: Series 7 by Arne Jacobsen. Folding table: Eiermann. Artwork: Jenny Holzer.

Max' Piano Bar
Villasimius, Sardinia, Italy

Architect: Pierluigi Piu
Client: Mr Giorgio Dessi. Main Contractor: Blindosider(building and metal works). Electrical

system: Renzo Palmas. Air-conditioning: Servizi Tecnologici. Ceilings: Sarda Metalprofili. Bar and kitchen fittings: Faticoni. Toilet walling: Bisazza. Lighting: Reggiani. Easy chairs: Xavier Pouchard (1934) re-edited by Fenêtre sur Cour.

Max Schmeling Sports Hall
Berlin, Germany

Architect: Joppien Dietz Architekten

Project team: Albert Dietz, Anett Eisen-Joppien, Jörg Joppien. Client: OSB Sportstäten GmbH. Structural and civil engineering: BGS Ingenieursozietät. Building services: Weidleplan Consulting GmbH. Building physics: Fraunhofer Institut fur Bauphysik. Energy conservation: IBUS Institut für Bau-Umwelt- und Solarforschung. Steel roof construction: BIT Spa-Stahlkonstruktionen. Interior glazing: Eyrich + Schindewolf. Façades and glass construction: Freiss Metellbau GmbH. Roof landscaping: Immo Herbst GmbH.

Media Plaza
Utrecht, The Netherlands

Architect: Sander Architecten

Project Team: Ellen Sander, Leontine Boots, Olga Gerretsen, Jan Klepper, Jeroen van Niewenhuizen, Bonne Plat, Jan van der Schaaf, Nicole van Slingerland, Baukje van der Steeg. Client: Stichting Media Plasa. Main contractor: Hollandsche Beton Groep. Construction: Pieters Bouwtechniek. Mechanical and electrical: Kropman BV. Lighting: Bossinade Lightworks BV. Furniture: CAR Industrie BV. Metallic mesh: LFC Lochem BV. Tiles basin: Intercodam Keramiek BV. Skybar: Meubelfabriek Schalkwijk BV. Shuttle: Varwijk Interieurbouwers BV. Tube: Bos & Van Rijs Staalwerken BV. Glass: Krug Kerrebijn BV.

Myoken-zan Buddist Hall
Kawanishi City, Japan

Architect: Shin Takamatsu Architect & Associates

Client: Kansai Sinnyoji Nose Myoken-zan. Collaborating Designer/Main Contractor: Toda Corporation (structural engineers). Mechanical engineers: Architectural Environmental Laboratory.

Nike Town
London, UK

Architect: BDP; Nike Retail Design

Project team: Nicholas Terry (BDP project director), Martin Cook (BDP interior design and managing director), Stephen Anderson (project design team leader, BDP design director), Jack Hobbs (project team leader, BDP design director), Sarah Turnbull, Rachael Brown, Greg Holme, Angela Beesley, Wynne James, Christopher Lenane, Adam Woof, Ian Fisher, Carla Montague (project secretary). Nike design team: John Hoke, Jerry Conduff, Tom Mulvey. Associate Designers: Electrosonic Ltd. (audi-visual); Client: Nike Retail bv. Main Contractor: Kvaerner Trollope and Colls. Building services: Lorne Stewart. Metalwork and joinery: Trollope Colls Elliott. Theatrical lighting: AC Lighting. Partitioning: Boler and Clarke. Stock storage system: Penwright. Stock transport system (shoe tubes): Telelift (UK) Ltd. Suspended ceilings: James Rose Projects Ltd. Clock

Feature: John Smith and Sons. Plaster: Armourcoat. Epoxy resin terrazzo floors: Fribel International. Rubber flooring: Dalsouple. Aluminium grate flooring: Eurotech. Paving: Charcon. Lighting: Concord.

One Aldwych
London, UK

Architect: Jestico + Whiles

Project team: John Whiles, John Wotton, Eoin Keating, James Dilley, Frank Reynolds, Andy Piles, Julia van Beelen, Julian Dickens, Laurence Osborn, Tony Ling, Anne Rowell. Client: One Aldwych. Main contractor: Bovis Construction. Project management: Dunraven Management Services. Interior planning: Jestico + Whiles Interiors; Sneiz Torbarina. Interior design: Fox Linton associates; Gordon Campbell Gray. Quantity surveyor: Gleeds. Structural and ME consultants: Cundall Johnston & Partners. Lighting consultant: Lighting Design International. Acoustic consultant: Hann Tucker. Ironmongery: Allgood. Stainless-steel mesh panels: Bassett & Findley. Light fittings: Absolute Action. Mosaic tiles: Bisazza Mosaico. Etched glass: Nero Design.

Rehabilitation Clinic and Health Spa
Bad Colberg, Germany

Architect: Kauffmann Theilig & Partner

Project Team: Manfred Ehrle (project architect), Michael Stikel, Lucas Müller, Annette Höftmann, Katrin Stein, Elmar Holtkamp. Client: Bad Colberg Kliniken GmbH. Building Physics: Transsolar. Planning: Weischede and Partner. Electrical consultant: Falk & Partner. Electrical engineering: Dess, Falk & Partner. Urban design: Kauffmann Theilig & Partner; Luz & Partner. Structural engineer: Weischede & Partner. Spa equipment: Ebert Ingenieure.

Reichstag Plenary Building
Berlin, Germany

Architect: Foster and Partners

Project team: Sir Norman Foster, David Nelson, Mark Braun, Christian Hallmann, Ulrich Hamann, Dieter Muller, Ingo Pott. Client: Bundesrepublik Deutschland. Site supervision: BAL AG. Structural engineers: Leonhardt Andrä & Partner; Ove Arup Partnership, Schlaich Bergermann & Partner. Acoustics: Müller BBM GmbH; IKP Ingenieur Büro Knothe; Prof Dr. George Plenge. M&E services: Kaiser Bautechnik Ingenieurgesellschaft mbH; Kuehn Baur Partner; Fischer – Energie + Haustechnik; Amstein + Walthert; Planungsgruppe Karnasch-Hackstein. Lighting consultant: Claude Engle. Conservation consultants: Acanthus. Cladding consultants: Emmer Pfenninger Partner AG. Building physics: Müller BBM GmbH.

RLB Citybank
Innsbruck, Austria

Architect: Peter Lorenz

Project team: Raimund Wulz, Manfred Konig, Martin Franzmair. Client: Raiffeisen Landesbank Tirol. Building contractor: Inneressner & Mayer. Structural engineer: Christian Aste. Electric installations: Fiegl & Spierlpoerger. Heating, sanitation and ventilation:

Stolz. Glass: Fa Spechtenhauser. Glass sliding door: Fa Manet. Metalwork: Fa. Dekassian. Terrazzo: Fa. Ebensperger. Lighting: Halotech. Carpets: Fa. Engel. Stonemason: Fa Rauth. Carpenter and furniture: Fa. Kuen. Artworks: Brigitte Kowanz (lights over entrance and clocks); Eva Schlegel (glass etchings). Light consultant: Concept Licht.

Roger Williams Hotel
New York, USA

Architect: Rafael Viñoly Architects

Project team: Rafael Viñoly (principal), Diana Viñoly (project designer), James Herr (project manager), Portia Fong (project architect), Maria Rusconi (staff architect), Andres Batista. Client: the Gotham Hospitality Group. Main contractor: Vanguard Construction. Structural engineer: Severud Associates. MEP/fire protection: Flack & Kurtz. Interior contractor: DJM. Lighting: Syska + Hennessy; Hillmann Di Bernardo (designers); RAB; Atlite; Halo. Lamps: TSAO+CLS. Plumbing contractor: RNA Mechanical Maintenance. Mechanical contractor: Jamco Air Conditioning. Electrical contractor: QNCC Electric. Graphics: Rick Henschel Design. Chairs and stools: Rae Trading Corp. Lounge furniture: Scoblick Brothers. Dining room table: James Hepner. Dining room shelving: B & Z Shelving; McNichols. Leather: Cortina. Area rugs: Sherland and Farrington. Flooring: Delta Polymers; Deborah Flannery. Maple flooring: Haywood + Burke (hardwood lobby); Permagrain Timeless Series (corridors). Bar: Demogod Inc. Panel fabric: Rose Brand. Custom zinc metalwork: Anthony Carta Speciality Metals. Glass railings: Julius Blum. Limestone: Urban DC. Carpet: Fortune Contract (rooms); Masland (lobby); Popular Carpet. Tibetan Rugs: Odegard. Shoji Screen Fabric: 'thinsln' fiberglas. Bathroom counter: Brazilian Slate. Bathroom tiles: Gascogne Blue Limestone. Custom bathroom glass: Checker Glass.

Ruskin Library
Lancaster University, UK

Architect: MacCormac Jamieson Prichard

Project Team: Richard MacCormac, Peter Jamieson, Oliver Smith, Toby Johnson, David Bonta, Glaspole Graham, Rainer Hofmann, Jessie Marshall, Pal Sandhu. Client: Lancaster University. Main contractor: John Laing Construction. Quantity surveyor: Gleeds. Structural engineer: Harris and Sutherland. Consulting engineer: Peter Deer Associates. Landscape architects: Cambridge Landscape. Gallery fitting-out, bronze lights and feature doors: A. Edmunds & Company. Steelwork: F & J Hauk. Windows: Bacup Architectural; Schuco International. Mechanical subcontractor: Haden Young Limited. Electrical subcontractor: ABB Stewards. Specialist plaster: Ashok Specialists. Archive framing and other joinery: Stockport Joinery. Roofing: Kershaws. Blockwork: Lignacite. Purpose-designed furniture: Peter Hall & Son.

SAS Radisson Hotel
Copenhagen, Denmark

Architect Mahmoudieh Design

Project Team: Yasmine Mahmoudieh, Albino Cipriani, Stephanie v. Kuzchenbach, Christoph Hildebrand, Olaf Koeppen. Client. Radisson SAS. Engineering: Radisson. Furniture: Yasmine Mahmoudieh, Antonio

Citterio. Acoustic material and carpentry: Hagendorf & Sichmann. Laminates: Abet Laminati. Fabrics: Kvadrat Bolig Textiler. Carpets: Ruckstuhl. Lighting: Tobias Grau.

Soho Brewing Company
London, UK

Architect: BOA (Barber Osgerby Associates)

Project team: Edward Barber, Jay Osgerby. Client: Soho Brewing Company. Main contractor: Constructive Interiors. Subcontractors: Westcrete. Structural engineers: Pryce and Myers. Brewing consultants: Caspary Schultz. Lights: Sill Lighting. Furniture: BOA (design), Windmill Furniture (manufacture).

Space NK Apothecary
Manchester, UK

Architect: Virgile & Stone Associates Ltd

Project Team: Gillian Brown (project team leader), Anna-Louise Thomas (business development), Moira Crichton, Beth Eyre. Client: Space NK Apothecary.

Spencer Theater for Performing Arts
Ruidoso, New Mexico, USA

Architect: Antoine Predock Architect

Project team: Antoine Predock (principal-in-charge), Geoffrey Beebe; Douglas Friend (senior associates-in-charge), Jorge Burbano, Devendra Contractor, Mark Donahue, W. Anthony Evanko, Paul Gonzales, Thea Hahn, Georgina Kish, Jennifer Lein, Robert McElheney, Lawrence Mead, John Morrow, George Newlands, Hadrian Predock, Kira Sowanick, Michele Cohen, Deborah Waldrip. Client: Spencer Theater. Main contractor: PCL Construction Services Inc. Structural engineer: Paragon structural design, Inc. Mechanical and plumbing contractor: P2RS Group Inc. Electrical engineer: Telcon. Theatre consultant: Fisher Dachs. Acoustics: McKay Conant Brook. Lighting: Lighting Design Alliance; Alexis Friend (lobby).

TBWA/Chiat/Day
Los Angeles, USA

Architect: Clive Wilkinson Architects

Project team: Clive Wilkinson (design director); John Berry, Robert Kerr (project architects), Jane Wuu, Christian Bandi, Tom Nohr, Mark Hudson, Andrea Keller, Marni Nelco, Ho-Yu Fong. Client: TBWA/Chiat/Day. General contractor: Matt Construction. Project manager: Stegeman & Kastner. Structural engineer: John A Martin & Associates. MEP engineers: Syska & Hennessy. Lighting design: Joe Kaplan. General areas: Tent fabrication: J. Miller Canvas. Rubber flooring: Burke Roleau. Custom dyed carpet: Shaw Industries. Park furniture: Smith & Hawkin. Millwork: Daystar; Pat Abarta. *Nest* and *Hatchling* workstations: Steelcase/Turnstone (designed by Clive Wilkinson). Lighting in the Oz Conference Room: Fuscia, designed by A. Castiglioni and manufactured by Flos. Chairs in the boardroom: Onda, manufactured by Vitra. Surfboard bar: Spyder Boards. Bibendum chairs in the Gatehouse: Eileen Gray, manufactured by Palazzetti.

Time Beach Bar
Whitley Bay, UK

Architect: Paul Daly Design Studio

Associate designer: Ronaldo Masoni (shop fitting). Client: Ultimate Leisure. Poured flooring: Lasar Europe Ltd. 'Yoga' Beer font: Paul Daly. Specialist lighting: Jeremy Lord. Specialist wall finish: Lasar Europe Ltd. General lighting: Light Attack.

Torre Lazur Communication Wing
Parsippany, New Jersey, USA

Architect: Kiss + Zwigard

Project team: Laszlo Kiss, Todd W. Zwigard (partners-in-charge), William Neburka (senior designer), Todd Eisenpresser. Architect of record: AA Architectural Inc. (Albert Albu). Client: Torre Lazur Communication. Main contractor: Mac-K Construction Inc. Flooring: Allstate Rubber Corp; Duraflex Inc.; Shaw Industries (carpet). Walls: Claridge; Cyro Industries; American Acrylic Corp.; Homasote Company. Acoustic tiles: Tectum Inc. Furniture: ICF (executive, conference and guest chairs); Poltronova (lounge chairs). Lighting: Artemide (task lights); Foscarini ('Promenade' lighting).

Vau Restaurant
Berlin, Germany

Architect: gmp – von Gerkan, Marg und Partner

Project team: Meinhard von Gerkan (architect), Doris Schaffler, Stephan Schutz, Gregor Hoheisel (assistant). Associate architect: Gregor Hoheisel. Client: Quotec GmbH. Main contractors: Ruth Buhner (carpentry); Clic (furniture); Kölper (painter); Mactec; Hallotec (lamps); Arte Interior (interior works). Lighting: Conceptlicht Helmut Angerer.

Virmani Fashion Shop
Munich, Germany

Architect: Design Associates

Project Team: Stephan Lang, Uwe Binnberg. Client: Virmani Pradeep. Main contractor: Schreinerei Eham. Lighting: Catallani and Smith; Kreon.

Wool Exchange
Bradford, UK

Architects: Dempster Thrussell and Rae.

Project team: Paul Thrussell (scheme concept), Andrew Dempster (design/project architect),Gary Pitchford (assistant project architect). Client: Eric Wright Construction. Design and build contractor: Maple Grove Developments. Structural engineer: Jordan Pritchard Gorman. Service engineer: Hoare Lea and Partners. Shop fit-out: Waterstone's.

Yeung's City Bar and Restaurant
London, UK

Architect: Studio MG Architects

Project Team: John Grimes, Wilf Sinclair, Ian Sharkey. Client: Rocheway Ltd. Main contractor: Eurostar Contractors. Graphic designer: Sharkey for Studio MG. Nuansol polyurethane resin flooring: Lazar (Europe). Walls: FR Shadbolt & sons. Furniture: Arne Jacobsen chairs, Art-Zeta bar stools supplied by Subtle.

Index